Remin

By

David McBride

Text Copyright ®2015 David McBride

Publishing Copyright ©2015 Laurel Rose Publishing

Laurel Rose Publishing

www.laurelrosepublishing.com

laurelrosepublishing@gmail.com

ISBN-13: 978-1517302139

ISBN-10: 1517302137

Dedication

This book is dedicated to my Wife, Patricia, who is a true inspiration to me and all who know her. She stood by my side, (in good times and bad). And during my long and painful fight with throat cancer, when the doctor said I might not have a year to live (in the year 2000), she encouraged me to keep fighting and working. Her quiet, firm, daily, push helped me to stay the course, and in 2005 I was declared cancer free. Her Faith and convictions are real and deep. Not only is she my true love, but also my best friend, and favorite companion. Patricia is one of the smartest people I have ever known.

Patricia suffered the untimely and tragic loss of her younger sister, husband, father, only brother, and only child, "Andrea Aiken", she mourned, and grieved, then picked herself up and fought on.

In 2008 Patricia suffered a serious stroke, which would have left most people bedridden or in a wheelchair at best. With no use of her right arm and limited use of her right leg she began to rehab at once and learned to write with her left hand, and do most functions with her left arm and hand. Using a cane she began to walk every day till she was walking one (1) hour every day. She never complains about the hand life has dealt her. Sometimes she cries and has moments of depression, but they only last for a while, then she soldiers on. She will say "I will lie me down and bleed a while, then rise and fight some more."

She is the classic example of a Southern Lady, cultured, soft spoken, very well read, gentle as a lamb, until her turf or family is threatened or impugned, then she is a Tiger. She demands respect and will not see any of her friends belittled or slandered. Very few people are foolhardy enough to match wits with her more than once. She is known for her wit, knowledge, and artistic ability, such as flower arrangements, and interior decorating skills, and encyclopedic knowledge of old movies.

Patricia has encouraged me to write of my life and the people I have known, and has served as my "spell check" in all my writings. I thank her for all she has been to me for many years!!

Acknowledgements

I would like to thank my family and friends who encouraged me to collect some of my stories into a book form. I thank my sister, Mary Margaret Jones, for her work in editing and correcting my many, many errors of grammar and punctuation. I would send her a story and she would make suggestions and corrections and send it back while it was still fresh in my mind. She has been a great help and always offered words of praise and encouragement.

Many of my friends have asked me to collect my stories in one volume. And after overcoming my inherent laziness I decided to get started.

Thanks to Laurel Rose Publishing Co. here in Senatobia MS. for the help and advice they have given, they are offering a great service to any aspiring author, they have the expertise to get things done in a friendly and helpful manner, never being critical or judgmental.

About The Author

David H. McBride was born July 14, 1937, in Laurel, Mississippi, the eldest son of George Huff McBride, a Methodist minister, and Edna McSween McBride. Growing up he lived in Moselle, Vancleave, Mount Olive, and back to Laurel. He then lived for many years in Hattiesburg and Laurel, Mississippi: Hammond, Louisiana: and Destin, Florida. He and his wife, Patricia, have lived in Senatobia, Mississippi, for the past 25 years where he owned and operated an automobile dealership until his retirement in 2012.

The father of four children, David also has four grandsons, one granddaughter, two great-grandsons, and one great-granddaughter. His sons Douglas Sean (Doug) McBride and Gregory Allison (Gregg) McBride live in Laurel. His daughter, Kathleen McBride Gaines, lives in Madison, Mississippi. His oldest son, Wm. David McBride, is deceased, as is his step-daughter, Andrea Aiken.

One of five children, David's older sister, Martha Jean McBride Manning, is deceased. His younger brother, George Stuart McBride, is also deceased. His youngest sister, Mary Margaret Jones, lives in St. Francisville, Louisiana, and his youngest brother, Anthony M. (Tony) lives in Savannah, Georgia.

Both David and Patricia are avid readers who read four to six books every week. He has approximately 2,500 hardback and about 2,000 paperbacks in his personal library. A lover of classical music and opera, David has an extensive collection of classical piano and opera CD's. He also loves classic Rock.

David's great-grandmother was a Choctaw person, which spurred his interest in their history and lives. Having studied Native Americans for the last 40 years, he has a large collection of books on the subject. In 1999, he wrote a book entitled "A Brief History of the Native Americans of the Southeast USA," and makes talks to schools and civic clubs about various aspects of Native American life and their culture.

Another of David's interests centers around the War Between the States. He has a large number of books about it, and nine of his ancestors fought in the war. He is a charter member of Senatobia's Sons of Confederate Veterans chapter, the Sam J. House Camp #837. David frequently lectures to clubs, schools, civic groups, and historical and genealogical societies about the war and events in the war, such as the Free State of Jones and the impact the war had on our state and the home life of ordinary people during this time.

David has been a pilot since 1965 and loves airplanes and aviation. He built and raced cars on the circle tracks in the 60's and 70's, loves old cars and has restored many antique cars: old Fords his most beloved. He just recently sold his 1949 Ford that he spent years restoring to like-new condition.

He has also owned and rode motorcycles most of his life. His sons also rode and shared his love for motorcycles as well as Go-Carts. David still watches auto racing of all types. Sprint Car racing has always been a favorite.

An active member of the Episcopal Church, David has served twice as Senior Warden. He is a nearly 25-year member of the Rotary Club and has served as president of his Club. Active in all facets of Freemasonry, David is a 32nd Degree Mason: Past Master of Ebenezer Lodge #76, Senatobia, Mississippi: a York Rite Mason: a member of the A & A Scottish Rite of Freemasonry, and a Master Craftsman.

David has written many stories about his life and the interesting people he has known and has had stories published in a variety of magazines and journals, including a well-known magazine with nationwide circulation.

Table of Contents

About The Author 6

EASTER SUNDAY..14

PRISONERS OF WAR...16

THE BURDEN OF SIN 20

THE DRAG LINE 26

PETS 29

MORE ABOUT PETS..33

MY LIFE WITH HORSES 39

THE POOL HALL..48

THE PICTURE SHOW..52

THE SCHOOL BUS 56

THE MONKEY 60

THE LIGHT POLE 64

THE CROSLEY..70

TUFFY 75

MIKE THE KNIFE 79

THE TOUGHEST GUY I EVER KNEW 82

I LOVE OLD FORDS 87

ROCK AND ROLL...93

THE BOUNCER..98

THE RACE CAR 101

MY FRIEND BUBBY 106

MORE ABOUT BUBBY..111

THE GREAT DEER HUNT 114

MY LIFE WITH GOUT 119

FOOD..126

BAR-B-QUE 129

THE SNAKE HUNTERS 133

MONA 138

MR. BIG STUFF 143

INANIMATE OBJECTS..150

THE BAG LADY..155

THE IRONSIDES...161

THE WILD BLUE YONDER...169

SHINE 175

SOME THINGS I HAVE NOTICED IN THE LAST 78 YEARS.........................179

A BRIEF OVERVIEW OF ISLAM 181

A DAY IN THE PARK 188

A SAVAGE JOURNEY THROUGH THE SOUTH..190

SOUTHERN WRITING 101..199

SOME INTERESTING FACTS ABOUT OUR STATE.......................................204

SOME OLD SAYINGS..207

PEOPLE I'D LIKE TO MEET & HAVE A TALK WITH 209

A BRIEF HISTORY OF THE NATIVE AMERICANS OF THE SOUTHEAST 210

Chapter I 212

Chapter II 220

Chapter III 231

Chapter IV 237

Chapter V 242

Chapter VI 245

"I know that most men, including those at ease with problems of the greatest complexity, can seldom accept even the simplest and most obvious truth, if it be such as would oblige them to admit the falsity of conclusions which they have delighted in explaining to colleagues, which they have proudly taught to others, and which they have woven, thread by thread, into the fabric of their lives."

By Leo Tolstoy

Sunday Morning Coming Down

It's Sunday morning and the same old pews

Are all filled with the same old crews

Who will always argue their same old views

Sharing as a group only a closed mind

And all with some special axe to grind

Not willing to share that which is mine

Or open my heart to the message divine

EASTER SUNDAY

Growing up as a child of a Methodist minister in the 40's and 50's had some advantages, but just as often, there were disadvantages. As a consequence, I learned early in life that a low profile sometimes was a big help. I was very shy as a small child, thus a low profile was part of my persona.

My brother Stuart was two years younger, and a low profile was never a part of his thought processes. He was a chubby, happy little fellow who always had a big smile and loved everyone. Stuart had a stuttering problem until his teen years, when I guess girls and a social life made it go away. Only when under stress or anger would the stuttering return, and since Stuart grew to about 6-4 and 220 lbs and a great athlete, very few people would cross him and make him angry enough for the stuttering to return. But as a small child, stuttering was a real problem for Stuart at school, at church, and on the playground.

Most people in the South go to church on a regular basis and know that the date of Easter was decided by the Council of Nicea in 325 AD, and falls on the first Sunday after the first full moon on or after March 21, and cannot occur before March 22nd or after April 25th. So with this in mind, a Sunday School teacher one Easter Sunday morning about 1946, at the Mt. Olive MS Methodist Church, asked the class,

"How do we know when it is Easter?" As she brightly looked around the room, I quickly ducked my head and looked at the floor. I knew the answer, but was too shy to say so in front of the class.

Out of the corner of my eye, I saw my little brother Stuart waving his hand and grinning from ear to ear. The teacher, knowing of Stuart's stuttering problem and doubting that at age 7 he knew the answer, kept looking around the room. I kept my eyes on the floor and waited for someone to answer. When no one spoke up, I sneaked a peek and only Stuart with a waving hand and big grin gave any indication of wanting to answer. Finally the teacher gave up on anyone else, and said with a slight sigh, "Okay, Stuart, how do we tell when it is Easter?"

With a happy look, Stuart said, "Mmmmmmy ddddddaddy haas aaaa cccalendar!"

PRISONERS OF WAR

The first regional library serving Desoto, Lafayette, Panola, Tate and Tunica counties does a great job of helping the public not only with good library personnel and computers but with many programs of interest to the public. Recently I saw a newspaper article about a traveling exhibit, sponsored by the library, about German prisoners of war held in the USA during World War Two. This exhibit was in a bus that had been modified into a rolling museum, with audio and video narration and exhibits and artifacts, all free to the public.

As I stepped onboard the bus and saw my first introductory panel and listened to the narration, a flood of memories washed over me. Long submerged and pushed aside, these memories were so strong that I felt a moment of dizziness; a backward step in time so vivid that I felt almost in that time and place again.

My father was a Methodist minister. In 1942 he was sent to Vancleave, Mississippi to minister to a "charge" which was a way of saying he had four churches to attend to instead of just one.

I guess the war had so depleted the ministry that some places only had part time preachers. The main church and parsonage was in Vancleave right on highway 57 which went right through the middle of the town then Mount Pleasant out East of town about seven or eight miles past the creole school.

Then he had Red Hill which was a smaller church, north and west, then Bonnie Chapel north and east, way off the main road. Needless to say my father was a busy man, preaching about seven sermons a week and doing a lot of going to and from these little churches.

Sometime in 1943 or 1944 a large German POW camp was set up at Camp Shelby just south of Hattiesburg Mississippi. Then a smaller camp was set up between Vancleave and Ocean Springs on the coast. During World War Two America imprisoned about 380,000 Germans, 50,000 Italians, and some 6 to 8,000 Japanese soldiers captured in combat and sent to this country to help with industrial and commercial labor. These prisoners were held in camps, and closely guarded by military people.

As I was about six or seven years old and full of curiosity I would sit and listen to adults talk about the war and listen to the radio broadcasts with my parents. Every newspaper and all the magazines my father read Life, Time, Saturday Evening Post etc. had articles and pictures of the fiendish Nazis, calling them Huns, bloodthirsty demons, and showing pictures of the beast like German soldiers killing men, women, children with no mercy.

One night long after dark a heavy knocking on our door woke us up. I followed my father to the door. Our porch was crowded with soldiers all armed with rifles and flashlights.

Several of the German soldiers had escaped and we were being told to keep on the lookout for them and lock all doors and report any unusual people in our area. I do not think our front door had a lock, and if it did we probably did not have a key for it. I wondered where a runaway German would go and what would he do in the great piney woods of south Mississippi.

The thought of all the ticks, chiggers stinging and biting, flies, mosquitos, and rattlesnakes should be enough to keep anyone safe inside the tents in the compound.

With the escape my curiosity knew no bounds. When the guards would march the prisoners up the highway to the big sawmill just north of us, I would hide in the ditch by the main road in the Gallberry bush which was very thick, and as I was quite skinny in those days I was completely hidden. I could hear the heavy *tramp tramp* of the marching men double timing around the curve before I could see them. I would hold my breath and not move till the Huns, escorted by the guards, were past me.

The first time I hid and watched I was astounded at the POW's. They were all fine looking men, straight and tall, no fangs dripping blood, no hunchbacks with long beards, no gross big belly monsters. Where were the Huns, the killers of women and little children? Sometimes they sang as they marched, though I could not understand the language I knew from the plaintive, slow tune that they were singing about home and family. One time the POWs stopped on the way back in the afternoon I was in my usual hiding place across from where they stopped for a rest and smoke break. I got a real close up look and could hear the small talk among them. They all looked so very much like us and spoke in soft tones to one another. The guards looked bored and tired. After about ten minutes or so the guards barked a command and the POWs put out the smokes and fell into formation. Some looked so sad with vacant eyes and no expression on their face, that I felt sad for them.

After about a year the POWs suddenly disappeared from our part of the world and then the war was over. For a while I would think of the so very young POWs and what a shock it must have been to be transported halfway around the world and set down in the piney woods of south Mississippi under guard 24 hours a day. In 1945 we moved away from that part of the state and I had forgotten about the POWs until this exhibit brought it back.

THE BURDEN OF SIN

Everyone who lives in the Deep South or has been raised in
the Deep South knows <u>SIN.</u> SIN is a part of our lives from
birth to death. We are reminded of our Sinful nature every
day of our lives.

Now, when I say Deep South, I am referring to that part of the
USA south of Memphis, TN, from Little Rock in the West to
south of Atlanta in the East and all of the Florida Panhandle,
but none of Florida south of Gainesville, none of Kentucky,
Tennessee, or any part of Louisiana south of Baton Rouge is
Deep South. Atlanta is not a Deep South city, nor is Nashville
or any part of South Carolina, North Carolina, or the
Virginias. The Deep South is separate and apart from the
Mason-Dixon Line, which only separates the North from the
textbook South. People who live up "Nawth" have no idea
what is Deep South.

We who live in the Deep South are reminded of our "Sin of
being Southern" every time we turn on the TV, every time we
pick up a national publication, whether it be a newspaper or a
slick paper publication like Vanity Fair or checkout line
garbage like People, US or other gossip rags, with absolutely
no redeeming social value!

CNN, ESPN, and all the "Network Pundits" with affected or real British accents remind us that we talk slow, walk slow, have accents, more than likely own firearms, go to church, do not rush around, and worst of all are descended from people who owned slaves, even though only a very small percentage of Southerners owned slaves, mostly purchased from merchants of Mass, Conn, and New York, but I guess selling slaves was not a Sin, only buying them!

Men in the Deep South were taught to stand when a lady entered a room, hold the door for her, never use bad language in her presence, excuse one's self when leaving a room or the dinner table. Violation of any of the above was a Sin, as was putting your elbows on the dinner table, chewing gum or wearing a hat in the house. Gossip was a Sin if done in a malicious way; however, among family it was not gossip, just keeping up with what is going on and who is straying from the straight and narrow path we heard so much about in church and from our mothers and grandmothers.

As the son of a Methodist minister in a small Mississippi town, I was under the microscope of the entire town. School teachers expected me to make all A's. Sunday school teachers expected me to know the answer to all Bible questions. Members of the congregation expected me to be the soul of decorum: polite, clean, respectful and most of all, free from wrong-doing. This was a heavy burden for a 9 year old boy.

Every Sunday morning, Sunday evening, and Wednesday evening we were in church, first Sunday School and then church services. My father preached about Sin. "All have Sinned and fallen short of the glory of God" all the time: Sins of Commission, Sins of Omission. Never did a Sunday or Wednesday service go by without a good dose of "The wages of Sin is death." This always scared me. I envisioned my Sins hanging over me and building up until they made a visible cloud hanging over my head for all the world to see.

After WWII, it took about a year for the economy to restructure and consumer goods to reappear in retail outlets, so in the fall of 1946, word spread like wildfire among the kids that a local store had received a shipment of firecrackers. No fireworks had been available during the war years, so this was big news in our little town. Every kid in town was scrounging around to get money to buy firecrackers, and I rushed to my father to ask for some money. In these years, ministers did not make very much money, and our budget was tight what with four kids to feed and my father's tendency to help every poor or distressed person who came by looking for help.

With this in mind, I very gently asked my father for a dime to buy two packs of firecrackers (5 cents per pack). "Did you finish mowing the lawn?" he sternly asked.

"Yes, sir, and I cut the weeds out back of the garage," I proudly added.

"Good," my father said. "Now, Mrs. Bailey (who lived next door) needs her grass cut." She was old and a widow and my father frequently volunteered me to assist her. "Cut her grass and I will give you the money for the firecrackers, though I consider it a waste of money."

Our lawn mower was old and a real chore to push. It was not gasoline or electric powered, but was a reel-type push mower, one-person powered, and I was a skinny, scrawny, nine year old. It took me two long hours to cut her little yard. Putting the lawn mower away and thinking all the while that all the firecrackers would be sold before I could get to town. I rushed in to my father for my money. Giving me the dime, he admonished me to be careful not to hold them in my hand, not to throw them at other kids, and not to place them in anything that would harm other people's property.

I took off running the six or seven blocks to downtown. Arriving at the store all out of breath, I saw other kids with firecrackers in hand. "Better hurry," they said. "They are running out fast." The firecrackers were sold by the lady who did the books in the back of the big store. Her office had a counter with latticework around it, one section of the counter folding up to gain access to her office. This lady went to our church, and so greeted me with a friendly "Hi, I guess you want some firecrackers?"

"Yes, ma'am, two packs please," I said, holding up my dime for her to see.

"I'm kinda busy," she said, "would you just reach in and get your two packs?"

"Sure," I said. She raised up the counter and pointed to a big box with Black Cat Fireworks printed on the front. I could see the box was almost empty. "Boy, that was close," I thought. Reaching into the box I picked up two packs of Black Cat, 25 count firecrackers, one with each hand. Holding them up for her to see, I put them in my pocket and headed out.

"Say hello to your folks and see you at church tomorrow," she exclaimed. "Yes ma'am," I replied.

As I started walking to the front of the store, I put my hand into my pocket to feel my firecrackers. "These packs sure feel thick," I thought. As I stepped outside into the sunlight, pulling out a pack for inspection I found that two packs had stuck together from the glue on the label having run, and I had two packs in each pocket. "WOW," was my first thought, "Four packs of Black Cat Firecrackers!" Then like a bolt of lightning it hit me. BUT I HAD ONLY PAID FOR TWO PACKS. I stopped dead in my tracks. I must go back in and tell the lady and give back the other two packs. Agony! Four packs versus two packs; twice the fun, twice the power, twice the experiments with blowing things up.

My first moral dilemma! What to do? What if she thought I stole them? Perhaps there were supposed to be two per pack. Naw! What if she saw me get two in each hand and was waiting to see if I came back and made things right? Or was waiting to tell my father if I did wrong or would do right? As I stood paralyzed with indecision, my pal Joe Russell, came running by shouting, "Come on, we are going to have a firecracker war behind my house." The thought of such fun outweighed the Sin of getting two extra packs for free, so I rushed off to join the firecracker war.

Next day being Sunday, I got up with the thought of my Sin hanging heavy over my head. I began to drag my feet getting ready, the thought of seeing the lady from the store almost too much to bear. "What is wrong with you?" my mother demanded to know.

"I just don't feel good," I managed to mumble.

"Well, your little sister has a bad cold. You just stay here and watch over her while we go to church. You take care of her and try to rest. Do not go out and play!" Well, even though I had a temporary reprieve, I was still in torment and worried sick about the firecracker deal. My Sinful burden was almost greater than I could bear. How could I ever face the woman at the store again? I would see her at church, on the street, at social gatherings, etc.

The Methodist Church solved my dilemma for me by reassigning my father to another town the very next week. As we were packing to move and saying our goodbyes, I would see the store lady, and every time, I would duck and dodge to make sure I did not make eye contact with her. It was years before I was able to push this episode far enough back in my mind to where the Sin would not grab me and torment me again.

THE DRAG LINE

When I was about twelve years, I would ride my bike all up and down the road we lived on and all over the area. It was not unusual for me to ride 10 miles or more in a morning's ride.

About a mile from our house towards Tallahala Creek was large clay mining operation. I would stop and watch the man operating the dragline. This big machine would swivel and cast its large steel bucket into the pit. Then, with a roar of the engine, the cables would begin to drag the big clam shell bucket towards it .then the boom would rise and lift a load of clay, and turn and deposit it into the back of a waiting dump truck. Then the process would start again. The ease and grace of the operation enthralled me. I would wonder how the man could stop the big bucket without a jerk or hitch just a foot above the truck so gently that not a rock would spill; then empty the bucket by tilting with the attached cables.

The bucket resembled a large steel bathtub with the end cut off and steel teeth on the bottom side to cut into the earth when the cable pulled it. The boom extended outward at a 45-degree angle from the cab where the man sat pulling on the levers. The boom must have been 50 feet or longer, and the bucket was dangling from the boom by the cables, I guess about another 30 or 40 feet or so.

The movement was so smooth it would not even quiver, so delicate was his touch. It seemed like magic to me, at my 12 years of age. There was never a wasted motion, never need to reverse or adjust the height or lateral placement of the bucket. I guess everyone likes to watch excavation in progress and a big hole being dug was of great interest to me. I would watch for hours.

One summer morning I decided to go watch the dragline in operation. My younger brother Stuart went with me to watch this fascinating deal. We arrived at the pit at about lunchtime. There were no trucks at the site and the operator was sitting on one of the tracks eating a sandwich. The man introduced himself to us. His name was Max Holifield, and as I was to learn in years to come, a real legend in his own time. Max Holifield was a pilot, and famous for his dare devil exploits. He was alleged to have flown through the Laurel Airport Hangar, both doors being open at the time. He was a motorcycle rider and hotrod mechanic of much renown. He had two good-looking daughters both of whom rode fast motorcycles as well as anyone. He could tune a racecar by ear, needing only a screwdriver. With his years of knowledge, Max would ride or drive or fly anything he could get his hands on.

After finishing his lunch, Max Holifield asked if we would like a Ride while he was waiting for the trucks to return? Unsure of what he meant I asked, "Ride"? "In the bucket", he said. "You boys get in the bucket and I will give y'all a Ride better than at he fair." After thinking about it for 5 seconds, I said to my brother "let's get in the bucket before he changes his mind!" Quickly we got in the big steel bucket. The sides came up to our waist, as we were not very big at the time. He climbed in the cab, and with a roar the diesel engine fired up. Without a jerk the cables tightened, and as smooth as an elevator we were suddenly 50 feet in the air. As effortless as a rock on the end of a piece of string he swung us around over the pit then raised and lowered us without a jerk. Then he changed directions and swung us full circle, then changed directions and swung us the other way. To say we were thrilled was a gross understatement. We were absolutely in boy heaven. Nothing prior to this could compare with our elation. Then without a bump, he gently lowered the bucket to within 6 inches of the ground. "Well boys, I guess I need to get back to work", he said. We got out thanking him profusely for the ride of our young lives. We got on our bikes, heading home.

As we rode toward home I began to think about our adventure. I did not think our parents would approve of our Ride, so we agreed not to share this with anyone.

For years to come when we would ride by this, or any such operation, Stuart and I would smile and nudge each other, but we never told our parents of the Ride.

PETS

We had pets around our house as far back as I can remember. In fact, one of my very early memories is about some goldfish we had in our living room swimming in a little glass fishbowl. I must have been about age five, because my little sister was a little baby. We were living in the parsonage of the Crossroads Methodist Church, just west of Moselle, Mississippi, where my father was the pastor. It was very cold that winter, and we had little heat in the house. Several pot-bellied wood heaters were the sum total of the heating system, plus the kerosene stove in the kitchen.

Bright and early one very cold morning, I was up stirring around the house, when I wandered into the living room and discovered the goldfish frozen in the clear water. One of the four little fish had his head out of the water, frozen solid. This was a new experience for me, so I began to examine the scene. I waked my older sister, who was two years older, to get her opinion. When she saw the little dead fish, half in and half out of the water, she began to weep and wail, and ran in and waked up our mother, who came in and looked aghast at the pitiful little fish. "Well," she said, "I think this little fellow is done for, but I have heard that some fish will survive a freeze if thawed slowly." So into the kitchen we go. Mother lights the cranky old stove, places the fishbowl in a pan half-filled with water over low heat, while we all stand and stare; after some 10 to 15 minutes, the water in the fishbowl began to thaw, and lo and behold, the three little goldfish began to quiver, convulse, and come to life. All three survived to swim some more. I do not remember what became of them after that, as I lost interest and found new playthings.

We always had a dog or cat around the house. NEVER IN THE HOUSE, as animals did not live in the house! We never bought a dog or cat. Someone would give us a puppy or kitten, or one would just wander up. We would feed it some table scraps and chicken bones out by the back door, and the dog or cat would take up residence and become OURS. They would live under the house, or in the garage or outbuilding, or just in the woods, usually giving birth to a litter, which gave us something to do playing with puppies or kittens. We never took an animal to the vet. In fact, I do not remember a vet until I was about grown.

I never had a dog that could not find its way home for meal time. My old dogs would follow me into the woods and swamps, sometimes taking a different path and not see me again until dark when I would go to the back door where we had an old Ford truck hubcap for a food dish. Rattling the spoon against the heavy metal hubcap always brought my old dog running up, tail wagging, jumping around, ready to eat whatever we had left over. I never had any animal indicate that he or she did not like what we served: peas, beans, cornbread, all leftovers were eaten and the hubcap licked clean! No animal ever thought about coming in our house, at least not after the first attempt, when my mother would flail at them with a broom and shout, "And stay out!"

I always had cats and dogs around, and felt at home with them as companions. I even had an old Red Bone hound once that would heed a command, "Come, Sit, Shake hands, Sic 'em," etc. When he just vanished one day, I missed him for a few days until I got another. I knew my dogs were not human and could not answer me when I said, "Come here," or "Sic 'em."

Today I am amazed at the number of people who have animals living in the house with them and seem to think that the animals are somewhat human. They are afraid the animal will get outside and cannot find its way home. What's up with that? Does it not know who feeds it? Is it that stupid that it does not know where its trained human, who caters to its every whim, is? I see some animals carried around like a baby, with little sweaters if it gets cold weather. Do people not know that dogs are descended from wolves and can fend very well for themselves?

Worse are people who own invasive species, like the Burmese python, that now is a threat to all wildlife in Florida and will spread to be a threat to the Southern USA. These strange pets seem to satisfy some longing to be different. Big hairy spiders for pets? Snakes? Rats? Fish that will bite you or poison you, as the lion fish, now a threat off the coast of Florida, a native of the South Pacific. Some nutcase brought some to Florida and a hurricane set them free. Now we have to worry about a poison fish, for crying out loud!

I see people kissing dogs and some cats in the mouth. These people will say, "Oh, a dog's mouth is just as clean as a human's." BS! All veterinarians and all studies show that animals have nasty mouths and spread bad germs and spread diseases to humans that can even kill. Besides, any animal that wipes its rear end with its tongue and its best friends rear end, does not get a kiss from me!

I would not mind having a dog around to chase the squirrels and chipmunks away from my veggie garden and to be glad to see me when I get home, but what do you do with a dog when you decide to go visit your brother in Savannah, Georgia, or take a vacation in Florida and will be gone for a week or so? A dog in the car for a long trip is out of the question, and boarding the dog is not fair to it. I am uncomfortable with a dog or cat in the house. Hair, dander, fleas, ticks, germs, etc., so I will just pet and stroke other people's animals and watch people carry on about their pets and try not to think about them letting Fido or Fluffy lick and kiss them in the face, just after watching said animal licking and kissing its own rear.

MORE ABOUT PETS

Several weeks ago, I wrote a little story about pets and the interaction of animals, and the humans who claimed to be the owners of same. I have been amazed at the response I have received: several phone calls (most long distance), several texts, many e-mails and personal contacts. One lady even wrote in cursive, via U. S. Postal Service snail mail. At church, civic clubs, and even at Wal-Mart, people have commented. While most of the feedback has been very positive and supportive of my position, a few seem to think that I am anti-animal or anti-pet. This is absolutely not the case. A little background follows.

As a child, we always had cats or dogs around, as I said before, and we just accepted the fact that they were animals and not humans. About the time I was in junior high, my paternal grandmother came to live with us. She was a dear sweet, gentle person and we all loved her. My father built a room and bath on the house for her, and she began to settle in. One minor problem: she had a beautiful long-haired, blue Persian cat. It really was a blue color. This cat was her pride and joy and slept beside her bed. My mother had always had a hard and fast rule: no animals in the house! This cat was so regal and so beautiful that she won my mother over, so the cat moved in. We all fell in love with this animal. My Granny called her "Old Sister," even though she was quite young. Old Sister was a very polite, clean, quiet thing. When she got

ready to go outside for personal duties, she would come to a
room where people were, walk to the door, look at the nearest
person, meow, and look back at the door and wait for the door
to open. If ignored she would repeat. If still no results, she
would slowly walk to the nearest person, tap them on the leg
or arm, firmly, and then go back to the door, looking back
over her shoulder and meow again, this time loudly. She
never failed to go outside, rain or shine!

Sometime after moving in with us, Old Sister had a litter of six
kittens. Four were blue Persian carbon copies of herself, the
other two somewhat nondescript and ordinary looking. These
two were given away early on. The others were raised and
given to friends and relatives who would appreciate and care
for them. For some reason, long-haired Persians are just
different: very calm, very much in control. They seem to
think each situation out before acting, never get nervous or
run around aimlessly. Old Sister lived to be very old and died
about the same time Granny did.

Having broken the taboo against animals in the house, my
younger brother brought home a Manx cat that was a gift of a
friend. For those not familiar with the Manx, it is a large cat
with a bob tail and a big head. The hind legs are longer than
the front, which gives it a strange rakish air, like a hot rod
ready to drag race. This was a big cat, even though just a
kitten, looked like a solid black bobcat, and had a strange
howl, not a meow, more like a screech owl. It being solid
black, my brother named him Lucifer, as he was black as coal

and just as uncooperative as a cat could be. Nothing suited
this cat. If he was inside, he wanted out; if he was outside, he
wanted in, and would give out a howl that would wake the
dead! Woe be unto any dog that wandered up in our yard.
Lucifer would hide and then pounce on the poor unsuspecting
thing with a howl that curled your hair. Lucifer always
attacked the dog's head, and being so big, the fight was over
before it really got started. One of our neighbors had two
coon hounds that were very big and mean. One day they
wandered up, not knowing that Lucifer was about eight feet
up in a small oak tree by the house. When the hounds got
underneath, Lucifer dropped like a bomb on the lead dog's
head, screeching and clawing with all four feet. Those two
dogs never came near our house again! The owner came over
to see what had done such damage to his hound dog's head.
He left, shaking his head and mumbling about that "wild,
black thang" we owned.

Early one winter morning, Mother walked into the kitchen
and lo and behold, lying by the stove was Lucifer and a tiny,
solid black kitten, fresh born. Lucifer was looking at the kitten
as if he had no idea what was going on or why. Just one little
black kitten. It only lived a day or so, as Lucifer ignored it and
acted like this was not of his doing. Mother tried to nurse the
little thing, feed it, etc., but I guess with no mother, it just
died. Now this was a shock to all concerned as all of us had
just assumed that Lucifer was a male. It was given to my
brother as a male, so named Lucifer and addressed as "he."
Since we now had proof that he was not a he, a conference

was held, and he was renamed Lucy. Lucy never had any more offspring, lived to be the very old age of 19 years; we know when we got her and know when she died. Lucy was a holy terror all her life. She hated little children and always tried to scare the toddlers, would screech and yowl whenever little ones were around, and would claw at you when you tried to put her outside. It got so bad in her old age, that she was banished to the garage when company came, if there were kids. No one dared bring a small dog around. Lucy would swell up like a wild cat and attack on sight. When Lucy just lay down and died one day, we all had mixed emotions.

When my children got to the age when they wanted a pet, I got a Springer Spaniel puppy from a friend that was raising hunting dogs. I planned on killing two birds with one stone on this deal, a gentle well-bred dog for the kids' pet, and, as I was doing a lot of dove and quail hunting at this time, a choice dog for me. This dog was from a long line of hunting dogs and bred to fetch and retrieve. This would be ideal. I would take the dog hunting, easing my burden on dove hunts, quail hunts, duck hunts, etc. Gleefully, I began to make plans to train this dog. His name on the papers was something long and complicated, had royal highness something or other of Kerry, yada, yada, so we named him Kerry.

Kerry was a beautiful brown and white, bright and alert, seemed eager for training, so I started in by bringing home some dead doves and teaching Kerry to fetch and spit them out by my leg. All went well until the day I took the shotgun and threw a dead dove out and fired a shot and said, "Fetch!" Looking around, I could not find Kerry. Where was my loyal companion and prized hunting dog? Kerry could not be found. As I walked back to the house, puzzled by this turn of events, I saw Kerry cowering under the back steps. I called him out, and he came slinking and groveling, chin on the ground. What the @#& was going on! With Kerry slinking at my heels, on a hunch, I turned and shot straight up into the trees. In a flash, Kerry was back under the steps, shaking and acting like I had shot him.

I could not believe I had the only gun-shy Springer Spaniel in the world. These dogs are famous worldwide for their hunting and ability to retrieve under all conditions. I tried to have Kerry trained by people who knew about this sort of thing, all to no avail: no luck. Kerry got so attuned that I could pick up a gun and he would hide for hours. Once to show a friend, I loudly said, "Kerry, want to go hunting?" He nearly tore the door down getting out to hide. Oh well, he made a great pet for the kids. One day a neighbor's kid threw a firecracker, not at Kerry just in the general area, and Kerry panicked and ran into the street and was killed. No one could ever figure out why this dog was so afraid of any noise that sounded like a gunshot.

My children had other cats and dogs around for years and took care of them, nursed them, etc. One hot, summer afternoon, I came home and found my daughter with tears in her eyes. "Daddy, Daddy, Fluffy is up one of the pine trees and cannot get down." Fluffy was a cute little half-grown kitten, snow white and blue eyed. I walked outside and sure enough, Fluffy was about 25 feet up a pine tree on the bottom limb, meowing pitifully. "She cannot get down," my daughter cried. "What will we do?" After thinking about this a moment and looking at how high the cat was, I sat my daughter down and said, "Honey, I have never seen a cat skeleton in a tree, so cats will figure out a way to get down. After all, she got up there!" Much crying, mean old Daddy will not help, tears, frowns, scowls, etc. later, as we were eating supper, we all heard a loud meowing at the door. Sure enough, Fluffy had made it down.

My kids had many dogs and cats. My oldest son had a German Police dog that was the smartest dog I have ever seen. This dog seemed to be able to communicate with my son at a level I could not understand. Without a spoken word, the dog would get up and head to the door when my son was ready to go. Before a sound had been made, when the dog was outside and my son decided to leave, the dog would be waiting at the car, and not before.

I understand the love some people have of animals and the companionship they offer, yet they still are not human and cannot be made into humans. And I still am not going to kiss anything that wipes its own rear end or its friend's rear end with its tongue.

MY LIFE WITH HORSES

Growing up in small towns in Mississippi I was always exposed to horses, mules, Shetland ponies, donkeys, etc. One of my early memories is of a neighbor sitting me up on a Shetland Pony, so my Mother could take a picture, the whole time I sat there, the sneaky Pony was trying to reach around and bite me, Aw, he just likes to play like he will bite, the owner said, with a cruel laugh, but I knew the crafty Beast was doing everything in his power to bite me on the leg, So it was about age four that I learned how devious and treacherous equines are.

About age six or so a neighbor, a kid of about ten or twelve had a small spotted horse that he rode with utter abandon all over the neighborhood, one day I was playing marbles with several lads and up rode the horseman, getting off he began to tease us young boys, bragging about his ability to ride and our not being able to, for some reason I piped up and said I could ride if I had a Horse! Quickly the older lad took the challenge. "Get up here", he said "and show us how you can ride!"

Not wanting to back down in front of my buddies, I, with his help, got up on the horse. Sitting there, I was just starting to say, "see I could ride if I had a horse", when the older lad, shouted, HAAA and hit the horse across his backside with a stick. In a flash the horse was running pell mell across the big yard. I was scared to death. Holding on to the saddle horn with a death grip seemed the only thing to do as I was being bounced all over the saddle because my legs were not long

long enough to reach the stirrups, suddenly the horse ran under a Holly tree with low hanging limbs, self-preservation instincts kicked in and I reached up with both hands and grabbed a limb, in an instant I was hanging four feet off the ground and the horse was running down the street, with the owner chasing him, I dropped to the ground and ran home to hide from the irate owner.

My Grandfather was a farmer and always had several mules and a horse or two, one of the mules was very large, and Granddaddy called him Big Jack, a smaller one was called Little Jack, I do not remember the horses names. Big Jack could pull or haul anything on the place, and did all the heavy work, but was very difficult to work with.

Granddaddy complained about Big Jack being so stubborn and hard headed, one day I was in the hayloft playing cowboys and Indians when Big Jack wandered into the Barn, I had Just seen a Movie where the hero, Sunset Carson, or Wild Bill Elliot or Tex Ritter had made good his escape by dropping on to a horses back, from a hay loft, for some reason this seemed like the right time to try this foolish stunt, quickly I got position at the hayloft end, and when Big Jack walked back outside, I squatted down and jumped the few feet down onto his broad back, I had no idea that something so big and usually so slow could react so quickly, before I could think of a dismount plan , Big Jack, crow hopped sideways for about 20 feet then with a humpbacked motion, launched me about 20 feet over his head, I landed flat of my back on a manure pile, and some hay , which probably saved my life and kept me from having any broken bones, after getting my breath I staggered away, mindful of Big Jacks baleful stare, I gave him a wide berth after this fiasco, and gave up trying to ride Mules. After having a horse try to pen me against the side of a stall and .squeeze the breath out of me, which scared me badly, I gave up on trying to ride anything, with feet and teeth.

On the other hand, my brother Stuart, always loved horses, and would go miles out of his way to ride a horse for an hour or so. Later in life, Stuart, always thinking of himself as a Country Gentleman, bought a farm of several hundred acres with barns, riding arenas, fenced areas, a lake, all the stuff you need, to feel like a rancher or horseperson. Right away he bought horses for his daughter to ride and jump in competition and traveled all over the country to watch her compete.

On one of my visits I noticed a little donkey wandering about, loudly braying and coming up to everyone as if it were a large pet dog or something, the donkey came up to me and began nuzzling and sniffing at my pockets. "He wants a treat," Stuart said, "just push him away, and he will leave you alone". Wrong Answer! The donkey bit my pants right where I keep my money, tearing my pants and getting a fold of skin from my hip in his massive teeth, bringing a howl of pain, and I reacted by hitting the donkey on his head which hurt my fist much more than I hurt him. Plus somehow in the melee the donkey managed to step on my foot, which nearly brought me to my knees in pain from the bite and the stomped on foot. I swore I would never come near an equine anything again without a gun to defend myself.

However, the best laid plans of mice and men, oft come to naught. While living in the State of Louisiana several years after the altercation with the donkey, one of my friends dropped by my home to invite us on a trail ride at a dude ranch near Picayune Mississippi. I quickly began to decline, citing how busy we were that weekend, when my wife, overhearing the conversation, chimed in. "No! We are not busy that weekend we would love to go, it just sounds great, riding horses all morning, to a lunch rendezvous by the river, then riding back that afternoon, then drinks and the ride home with friends. It just sounds wonderful," she gushed, "we would love to participate."

So faced with all this enthusiasm and not wanting to be an old party pooper and killjoy, I caved in and agreed to this all day "Trail Ride" outing in the wilds of Mississippi.

Arriving at the Dude Ranch in Hancock County Ms. way out from Picayune, in the real Piney Woods, we were shown the map of the ride and where we were to be for the lunch break, which was included in the deal, I was becoming more concerned as I kept seeing people on horseback sporting

42

about, cantering and rearing up and showing out for their friends, running short distances then wheeling about and dashing back to the gathering area. I began to ask, where were OUR horses? And which one was MINE, I need a gentle older ride, I explained to the guy who seemed to be in charge, I do not like horses, and horses do not like me, I have never stayed on horse more than 2 or 3 seconds, I firmly explained to this guy, Nonsense! He replied, horses do not like or dislike any one! But sometimes, horses sense if a person is afraid of then, and act differently around this person, Be that as it may, I grumbled, I need a gentle, docile, horse that I can straddle for the duration of this ordeal, then get off and go home!!

We got you covered he replied, we do this many times a year, and we have just the right horse for you, Soon we were all saddled up, my wife had a real pretty somewhat spirited reddish horse, mine was a mean looking smallish gray mare with a sullen air

About her, starting the ride, my mare would not move at all, giddy up, giddy up, I repeated several times as the parade of riders began to move along, kicking her in the ribs and shaking the reins finally got the obstinate old nag to move along, she trotted with a stiff legged gait that bounced me up and down, shaking me to such an extent that my vision was blurry and my stomach felt queasy, the several Bloody Mary's I drank for breakfast, and the Champagne Mimosas for desert, may have contributed to my stomach unease, unable to take this punishment any longer I pulled back on the reins to slow down this unbearable bouncing, whereupon the vindictive beast just stopped, rearing her ugly head up and down, and looking around at me with a slit eyed mean look., by this time the caravan had moved on and I was about a thirty yards behind the group, I got her going again by kicking her ribs and shaking the reins, which produced the same bone jarring effect, so here we go, dead stop, then a teeth rattling rack, dead stop, then bone jarring rack, now I am now fifty yards behind the group, my wife waves and cheerfully says "Come On, you are Getting Behind " I grit my teeth and shout, Go on I will catch up.

As the trail zigged and zagged through the Piney woods I totally lost sight of my group, since the trail was well defined I assumed the hateful horses knew where to go and I became just a unwilling, unhappy, and very hot hostage, all this bouncing and jarring, and liquid intake soon reminded me that I must stop and answer a call of nature. As this call became a matter of urgency, I began to look around for a likely spot. Seeing a big clump of Gallberry bushes off the trail a few yards, I managed to stop the beast, and dismount, tying the reins to a young Pine tree. When I returned to my only means out of this expedition, I untied the reins then started to mount up.

Holding the reins in my left hand I put my left foot in the stirrup, just as I put my weight down to swing over the saddle, the evil wench looked at me with a sideways sneer, then jerked to her right, and took off like Man-O-War out of the gate, holding the reins and only one foot in the stirrup the other still on the ground, I was hopping on the ground foot trying to get leverage to swing over, after a few Olympic sized hops I turned lose the reins, jerked my foot out of the stirrup, and with a string of profanity that would have done justice to any sailor, I screamed goodbye and good riddance you old Glue Factory escapee? May you rot in hell, or be sold to France, Where they eat horses!

Hot, tired, mad, not a clue where I was or where anyone was , I walked along cursing all things equine and wondering how anyone could walk in cowboy boots, which seemed to be bent on rubbing blisters on both my feet. Hobbling around a curve in the trail I came upon a lady standing beside a horse holding the reins and crying and cursing at the same time. "Madam," I said, "if you are cursing this horse I will be glad to join in? by the way, did you see a small gray devil, disguised as a horse come by here?"

"A few minutes ago, a small gray rider-less horse came trotting by" she said, "I tried to grab the reins but she shook her head and picked up speed. I can do nothing with this horse I was assigned. It will not obey any command and now will not let me get back on. I got off to ease a leg cramp, now when I try to remount he jerks and moves sideways and will not let me get back on."

Mad as I was, I felt relief. This will be my way out of the wilderness. "Madam, if you will let me, I think I can get us to somewhere."

"For God's sake do whatever," she begged.

Tying the horse reins to a tree I helped her up in the saddle then I got up. The horse did not much like this arrangement but tolerated it. I untied the reins and we headed down the trail. She told me of her life long dislike of horses and how she was coerced into make this trip by friends who think everyone loves horses, even those who say they do not!!

After 30 minutes or so of riding along we rounded a curve and there was the river bank; white sandbar, tables arranged, food and drink everywhere. Folks were having a great time laughing and talking, frolicking in shallow waters by the sandbar. "Hey!" my wife cheerfully exclaimed, "where you been? We have been here for some time!" Before I could say a word I saw my gray mare standing in the shade, eyes closed, dozing, oblivious to the wave of hatred I directed her way.

After eating and resting up some the caravan began to mount up for the ride home.

With much fear and loathing, I got on the horse from Hell. As we turned to the trail the trail master said, very calmly, "do not worry, all these horses know the way home, and they will be glad to get there, so do not be surprised if they pick up the pace somewhat."

"No one will be as happy as I will," I muttered under my breath, "I hope this nag runs all the way to the barn if only I can stay on the top side." Sure enough the trip back was much quicker and uneventful. All the horses were moving at a brisk walk. My ugly mare attained a pace I could live with. I just gritted my teeth and held on and tried to think pleasant thoughts of home and hot showers, and cold drinks, and never being in the proximity of a nasty stinking four footed evil scheming equine monster again!

On the ride home, my cheerful little wife, exclaimed, "what fun, we should do this again!"

"Not in this lifetime" I mumbled under my breath!!

THE POOL HALL

I have always liked pool and pool halls. Growing up as the oldest son of a Methodist minister, every small town we lived in had a pool hall. These places were "off limits" to kids so we naturally did our best to find out what was going on in these places. Usually, pool halls were upstairs or in a building where access was limited, so as pre-teens we would skulk around to see who came and went, trying to catch any glimpse of inside. But all we ever got was the soft, silky click of a cue ball striking then the satisfying plop of the ball falling into the leather-lined pocket. We could only guess at the arcane activities inside. Pool halls were very quiet, hushed places, almost reverent. No music or PA systems, no loud talking or laughing, only the smell of cigar and cigarette smoke, and always the faint smell of alcohol. Someone was always going and coming carrying ice and mixers.

After I got old enough to gain admittance (about 15 years old) I was hooked. Watching the guys at the tables, snooker and regular, mostly older men all smoking and drinking something; quietly shooting, chalking up, and very smoothly making shots that I thought impossible, all with no effort or exerting any wasted motion. Someone was always around to collect the money for each game and bring ice or beer or a bottle of whiskey, usually a half-pint.

A lot of money was bet on some games and guys would gather around a table when the stakes got real high. Sometimes a muted cheer went up when a very good shot was made or a game ending where the betting was heavy. Around the sidelines were always guys playing dominoes or poker with plenty of betting going on. Some domino games had more money on the tables than some poker games. This action went on from opening, usually about 10 am, until closing time which varied by town based on the local law. Some were operated as private clubs and opened and closed at will. Liquor being illegal in Mississippi at this time, and all pool halls having access to same was a clue to me that some skullduggery was involved. I never heard of a pool hall being raided or shut down over any violation.

Ellisville, Mississippi had a big downtown pool hall on the ground floor, and with Jones County Junior College being just down the street always was full. They had snooker tables and regular tables, with a room in the back for dominos and poker, but no alcohol was allowed: too close to the Jr. College. They sold tobacco products, soft drinks, and snacks. You had to hide your booze outside in your car and sneak out for a drink and be very careful, for the Ellisville cops were wise to the ways of college kids and were always snooping around!

Laurel, Mississippi had a fine group of pool halls: Moose Lodge, IOOF (International Order of Odd Fellows) in the center of downtown, Elks Club, VFW, American Legion, and two or three other pool halls that I cannot remember the

names of all upstairs. The bowling alley had tables and
several cafes/bars had a table or two out in the county. Most
juke joints had a ratty old table and a few crooked cues. There
was a huge contrast between the hushed atmosphere of the
pool halls and the noisy bedlam of a juke joint. Shouts, loud
music, fights, laughing, cursing, and rips in the felt of the
tables all diminished the style and feel of the game, not to
mention the danger of getting hit with a cue stick or a thrown
cue ball when the inevitable fight started.

Having always wanted a table of my own, and my kids
getting to Jr. High and pre-teen age, I used this as a rationale
to buy my own table and make a game room out of half of my
garage, making a ping pong table to fit on top of the pool table
so it could be converted at will for pool or table tennis. I
taught my four kids to shoot pool. They all liked it and
became comfortable with a cue in hand. My daughter really
became a good shooter until basketball and boys diverted her
attention to more worldly things.

For many years I had a table in my home and loved to shoot
but moving around from Mississippi to Louisiana, to Florida,
and back to Mississippi hauling a pool table around was just
out of the question. I have not shot in many years but still
have my favorite two-piece stick with its case on a shelf in the
closet. I should give it to somebody, but maybe someday I
will find a place to shoot or find it a good home.

In the mid-fifties, the big Baptist Church in Laurel, Mississippi
held a public burning of rock and roll music and records in

the middle of the street in front of the church. The police blocked off the street, a huge bonfire was built, and all were invited to bring rock and roll records and music to throw on the fire, especially Elvis Presley who was looked upon as the Anti-Christ by most preachers: a Royal Crown pomaded, wild-eyed twisting, gyrating monster who was leading the youth down the path of total and utter destruction. (Quite naturally, we were eager to follow, as fast as possible.)

The same Baptist preacher who organized the Rock and Roll, Music and Record Burning event was always preaching about the pitfalls of life and how we kids were just not doing right. One of his sermons about the perils of life still sticks in my mind today. He was speaking to a large school group when he uttered these famous words, "The Classic Example of a Miss-Spent Youth is a Girl that can Shoot Pool and Roller Skate."

THE PICTURE SHOW

Between the ages of nine and fourteen, candy bars and funny books (comic books to the unlettered) were not as important to me as the picture show. Movie theater buildings and the tales unfolding on the glittering screen were called picture shows in the late forties and early fifties in Laurel, Mississippi. Laurel, Mississippi had five, (count 'em) five picture shows plus three Drive Inn shows (with which we will deal later). Plus the Lincoln Theatre for Blacks down by the R.R. tracks.

The Arabian Theater was the uptown deal. All Moorish, Rococo, velvet drapes sweeping and as richly colored as rubies, and a roomy, full balcony located above. Behind the white balcony was a small balcony with a separate entrance for the Blacks. Current movies showed at the Arabian and the air conditioning always worked real good in the summertime.

Down the street was the Ritz Theater. With a small lobby and a very small balcony, the Ritz was cozy and intimate. The Ritz showed a lot of love stories and movies that very seldom interested me during these years. The movie Billboards out front showed men and women gazing intently into each other's eyes, to convey the message of the romantic epic that was shown inside. These advertisements only served to hasten my step on my way around the corner to the Royal Theatre.

The Royal Theatre was a veritable haven for young boys with a double feature every Saturday preceded by the serial, then the comedy, then the coming attractions, then two hours of Sunset Carson, Lash LaRue, Roy Rogers, Gene Autry, The Durango Kid, Etc. Etc, Etc. It was common for us to sit through the next showing in order to see all this magic again. All of this for twenty-five cents. Plus, of course, popcorn and cokes in you were lucky enough to have an extra dime.

Then on Central Avenue, by the tracks, and next door to the Coca-Cola Bottling Company, there was the Strand Theater. The Strand was a minor League Arabian. Not quite so large, slightly run down but still pretty sporty. The Strand showed not quite so new and re-run movies. When a new one came to the Arabian and you could not, or would not spring for the price of the Arabian, you could rest assured that in a few months it would return to Laurel and be shown at the Strand. However, on most Saturdays, they would show "shoot 'em ups" as my Father referred to this genre. These were the upscale westerns of Randolph Scott, John Wayne and Gary Cooper.

Stories and Cinematography were coming into a new age and we proved to be an enraptured audience (Before they were concerned about demographics or political correctness).

And then there was the Jean Theater, down the street and a step down the social ladder. Sandwiched between the Jean Coffee shop and Kress's, or as we said "the five and dime store". The Jean was small, cramped, and a little scary. My older sister had told me of large rats that plagued the place; she who would have never been seen in that place. There were frequent delays as the film or an image of it would wither and turn brown, curl and catch fire before our very eyes. These breakdowns would lead to all of us stamping our feet, whistling, catcalling, and booing.

The Jean was dirty and dingy and a large lady with an attitude problem maintained order. She carried a large flashlight with which she would strike you on the shoulder a crushing blow and then order you out with no refund of your money. This presented a fate worse than death because you then had to wait outside until the show was over and your brother or companions came out and your father came to pick you up for the ride home. And then you had to try to explain to your parents why you were outside all alone.

The Strand and the Jean charged ten cents admission for patrons twelve and under and twenty-five cents if you were over twelve years old. My brother Stuart was a healthy lad, and looked older than his years. Because of this the lady in the ticket booth at the Strand, in a fit of mean spiritedness would sometimes challenge his age. Whereupon I would attest to his age being 10 or 11 as the case would be. On one occasion the lady would flat not believe me and ruled no to the dime ticket. Whereupon I went and got my mother, who worked at the J.C. Penney Company just one block down the street. My mother, with fire in her eyes, told the lady in no uncertain terms that he was not yet 12 years old. She relented under my mother's indignation, but said, "Next time bring his birth certificate."

The next week we arrived loaded for bear, birth certificate in hand and gleefully handed it over. With a frown and a harrumph, she punched out the dime ticket. But said he still looked too big for a dime ticket.

No one was happier than Stuart was when he became twelve and didn't have to suffer the indignation of being hassled every time over the price of admission at the Strand Theater on Saturdays.

THE SCHOOL BUS

All my Senior Year of High School I smelled of gasoline. My breath smelled like gas, my clothes smelled like gas, my car smelled like gas. Everything I owned smelled of gas. Although this sounds unusual there was a good explanation; it was the fault of the State of Mississippi. It was a clear-cut case of full liability on the part of the State.

Sometime in the 1940's the State of Mississippi, for some unknown reason, lost its mind and began to employ high school boys as bus drivers. No one in his or her right mind would have even considered this. Perhaps economic conditions of the times forced this State of affairs. I don't know the rationale behind this massive blunder, only the consequences.

Bus drivers were trained during the summer months, before school started in September. For some reason I cannot remember, I missed the Jones County drivers training school, and I had to take my training in Covington County, Collins, Mississippi about 25 miles away on Highway 84 West. So I had to get up very early and drive to Collins, Mississippi every morning for the training. Getting up early was a chore for me as I worked as a soda jerk at a place called the Frosty Treat in Laurel, Mississippi from 12 Noon until closing time, about 11 or 12 PM every day except Monday.

I loved working at the Frosty Treat because everyone in Laurel, Mississippi came by at least once a day, not to mention the 40 dollars a week I was paid for the approximately 60 to 70 hours I worked each week. At closing time, after clean up, I would hit the streets to find my buddies who were riding around town from place to place.

In the fifties all nice people were in bed long before midnight, so my friends were not always socially acceptable people. Certainly girls out after midnight were not the ones you bring home to meet your mother.

After getting home about two or three in the morning and grabbing a few hours sleep I would get up and drive to Collins, Mississippi for bus driver's school. My father had signed me up for this deal because he thought the discipline of the training would be good for me. I thought the Thirty dollars a month they paid was the real reason. (That's right, thirty dollars a month).

After finishing driver training and passing with an acceptable grade, I went to the bus barn at the Laurel Airport to get my bus with which I would haul about 50 or 60 kids to and from school each day. Being a Johnny come lately, I was assigned an old International bus with a weak six cylinder engine and a four speed non-synchronized transmission, which meant you had to be a master to change gears without horrible grinding sounds and hoots of derision from all who heard. Shouts such as "use the clutch, rookie" and other less flattering remarks about your ability to drive.

The fact that we kept the busses at our homes was the reason for my smelling of gas for a year. Every morning I made my route and picked up the kids then parked the bus at school until school was out then the return route letting off kids and then home.

Before you left school each afternoon, you made sure you checked the oil, water, etc, and then filled up with gas from the tank at the school if needed. The busses held about 25 gallons of gas and we filled up about every third day.

After getting home one Friday and considering the 25 gallons of gas in the bus and the one-gallon in my old Ford, and the lack of money in my pocket, the conditions were ripe for my transgressions. Finding an old garden hose and being an old hand at siphoning gas, I began to run the hose into the bus tank. My hose abruptly stopped about 6 or 8 inches down the filler tube. Taking the hose out, I peered into the tube and discovered a mesh screen made into the neck of the filler tube.

The bus maintenance men had been had been doing this a good while and obviously knew the mentality of boys. After thinking about it a few minutes, I got a hoe and jabbed the handle down the filler tube. Eureka! A neat hole in the barrier. Fetching my section of garden hose, I proceeded to siphon out a few gallons of gas into a container, getting it in my mouth and on my clothes in the process. After transferring it to my car, I tried to pull out my hose. Horror of Horrors, it would not come out! I pulled and twisted and pulled and sweated and cursed to no avail. It would not come out.

With thoughts of driving around with evidence of my guilt hanging out for all the world to see I became desperate. My Father was due home at any minute and he would not understand my stealing. In a fit of desperation, I took my knife and cut the hose off level with the neck, then took the hoe handle and pushed the hose into the tank. At that time, I could see the problem. When I jabbed a hole in the mesh, the crosspieces bent inward and would not let the hose back out.

With a sigh of relief I got in my car and went into town vowing not to run out of hose since it seemed I would sacrifice a six-foot piece every time I siphoned gas from the bus.

THE MONKEY

In my teen years my best friend, AG, was subject to disappear for weeks at a time. I never knew when he would appear on the scene. Usually it would be some night when I would be riding around aimlessly, as we were prone to do. We would drive up at Nubs or Judy's Drive Inn or some such late night place and there would be A.G. with a big grin on his face. "Hi cool" was his usual greeting. "What's cooking?" We would all ask "where ya been?" Oh around 'about, Houston, LA, or sometimes he would just ignore the question and say "let's have a beer" which was the end of that discussion.

One night as I was riding down Ellisville Boulevard going, I don't remember where, I met A.G. in his Ford Convertible. He blinked his lights and performed one of his famous U turns in the middle of the street, ignoring oncoming traffic. A.G. and I were known, in the local parlance, as "Hero Drivers" which meant we drove with a certain abandon, were blessed with a great deal of luck, were known for taking great risks, and earning the undying enmity of the Laurel Police Department. I pulled over in front of the icehouse and waited for him. When he pulled up, to my great surprise, A.G. had a monkey on his shoulder about the size of a big house cat.

The monkey had on a collar and was on a leash. The little creature clung to A.G. as if he were its Mother. It had a long tail and nearly human face. "For God's sake, where did you get the monkey?" I asked.

"Mexico" was the reply. "Ain't he cool, the little booger won't let go of me. He goes everywhere with me, eats French fries, potato chips and drinks cokes and beer. Pretty Cool, huh?"

"What do you plan on doing with him?" I asked.

"Hell, I just like him and I think he likes me. I think we suit each other, and I believe he will be a real girl magnet." This was music to my ears so I suggested we make the rounds of the night spots in search of girls. So monkey on A.G.'s shoulder we rode off in his Ford Convertible.

As we pulled into Nubs Steak House parking lot, we spied several girls that we knew in a big Buick, windows down to catch a breeze, and to ensure being seen. We pulled up beside them, and sure enough the girls all went wild over the Monkey. All four of them got out squealing and oohing and ahhing. "Oh, how cute, they said. Let me hold it." We got out of the car to get closer to the girls. Suddenly, the Monkey began to scream in a high shrill AIEEE, AIEEE, AIEEE, and clung to A.G. with all four feet and tail. When a girl would reach for it, the poor thing would go wild with what appeared to be total fright. "Maybe it don't like girls," was my observation. "Damn, said A.G. it sure looks like it. I was counting on the monkey to help out my love life!"

In the interest of pure scientific experimentation, we began to approach every woman we saw and without exception, the monkey would absolutely pitch a fit until the woman was at least 20 feet away. I guess this was considered a safe distance in monkey world. After about 10 experiences with women, we concluded that this monkey just flat did not like women,. so with this conclusion, we went on with our life and A.G. left the monkey at home if he planned to be around or pursue any women.

About 2 weeks later, A.G., the monkey and I were cruising the streets of Laurel on Easter Sunday. About 2 P.M. after everyone had been to Church, and had eaten Sunday dinner (as the noon meal was called in those days) we were riding down South Magnolia when we met a carload of girls. The driver of the car was a girl that A.G. had his eye on, and was trying to get a date with. Things had just not worked out as yet. With a blast of the horn and a big wave the girls had our full attention. With his usual aplomb, A.G. executed one of his famous U turns, totally disregarding all traffic and rules of the road.

We followed the girls to the Dairy Queen and pulled up beside them. We all got out and began to talk. A.G. left the monkey in the car, with its leash snapped to the steering wheel. One of the girls began to take on about the monkey. "Don't mess with the monkey, he don't like girls." A.G. said very firmly.

"But it's so cute", she said.

"Don't mess with the monkey, he don't like females." But she went right over to the car and picked up the monkey, it screaming bloody murder at the top of its shrill little lungs.

Unsnapping the leash from the steering wheel, and holding it to her shoulder she said "see, it just needed a firm woman's hand." At that exact moment, the pitiful little thing began to vomit down the back of her blue sun back Easter dress.

At the same time, its bowels turned loose down the front with an astonishing amount of smelly, green monkey shit, the poor horrified girl grabbed the monkey by the neck, whereupon it sank its teeth into her hand. With a scream of pain and horror she danced around like one possessed. A.G. quickly grabbed the terrified little thing and held it close. The girl just stood there, I guess in total shock, her hand bleeding, and her front and rear a stinking mess and all her friends jumping up and down screaming and crying. It was a real nightmare!

A.G. and I got back in his car and as we cranked up to leave; he looked at the wreck of a girl in her Easter Dress, and said, "I told you the monkey don't like girls."

THE LIGHT POLE

During my junior year of high school I acquired a new friend. His name was A.G., which stood for Archie George. Only a few people knew this and no one called him that to his face. He was simply A.G.

He came to Laurel from Burbank, California which was as distant as Hong Kong to us and was just as exotic. A.G. was not bothered by things like school or church or family. He lived with his grandmother out at Myrick and came and went as he pleased. No one seemed to be concerned with his life style or lack of home life or school, or church. He did not work and always had lots of money, a nice Olds convertible, a motorcycle, a hot rod, lots of clothes (jeans, leather jacket and tee shirts). A.G. had a tattoo on his right hand between the thumb and forefinger in the shape of a cross with lines radiating out from it. Years later I learned this was a gang identification. At the time I just thought it was quite sporty.

He and I became best friends in spite of his being not quite socially acceptable. One reason we became such good friends was our penchant for being out late at night. It was on one of these late night runs when A.G. suddenly stood up on the brakes in front of the Pan Am Service Station (a famous late night operation) and said, "Damn, there's my old man." I would never have referred to my father as "my old man."

Making a skillful, if somewhat loud U turn, we turned into the old Pan Am Service Station and Tire Recapping Facility. A.G. got out and walked over to a large, heavyset man and said "Hiya, Daddy O. I need some cash." With no show of emotion, the large man reached into his pocket and handed him a roll of cash. "New car?" A.G .asked, motioning to the brand new 1954 olds two tone blue and white hard top the man was leaning on.

"Yep", he replied and "keep your ass out of it."

"Come on, Daddy O, let us take it for a spin." A.G. asked with no trace of whining or begging in voice.

"Well," was the reply, "once around the block. But just once. I have a date in a few minutes and I don't want to keep her waiting." With a big grin, A.G. motioned for me to come on. We jumped into the new car, and with tires squalling. We shot out of the Pan Am, though the 5 way stop and roared up the hill towards Smith's Bakery and the bus station, then turned South toward town doing about 65 miles an hour on South Magnolia.

I somewhat quietly said, "We should go back. He said once around the block."

"Naw", A.G. said he will just chew us out when we get back. He ain't gone do nothing else." So we just rode a while showing off to our buddies, spinning tires, and wishing we could see some girls to take riding.

When we got back to the Pan Am about an hour later, the man was fit to be tied. He screamed and yelled; "you punks have made me late for my gal. I ought to kick your ass right now." I was scared as I could be.

A.G. just said, "Nice car Pops. Thanks for the ride. Are you going to be around here long?"

The man yelled a stream of profane words and said, "Go to hell. I may or may not be around!"

A.G. just said, "see ya Daddy O" as we got in his car and drove off.

I was puzzled about this and asked, "had you not seen your Dad in a few days?"

"Ha, a few months" was the reply. "I never know when I will see the old bastard, so I always hit him up for some dough. Let's see how much I got." Pulling out the roll, he counted it. "Two hundred, the tight old bastard," he said. At the time, I was working at the Frosty Treat after school and driving a school bus to earn dating and party money. I was lucky to earn $150 dollars a month total!

About a week after this incident, I was at work at the Frosty Treat Drive In about 10 P.M. when a friend came by and said, "have you heard about A.G.?"

"No, what do you mean," I asked.

"Well, he and his date were coming down South Magnolia headed this way when A.G. ran up on the sidewalk in front of the Orman's house and hit a light pole. Clipped that sucker off level with the ground. Then the pole fell on A.G.'s car, wires and all. Sparks were flying, people screaming, cops and ambulances were everywhere."

"Were they hurt?" I asked.

"Naw, the girl got bloody nose, A.G. got a bump on his head about the size of a golf ball. But the car is totaled. Just a pile of junk!"

The next day, after school, I arrived for my shift at the Frosty Treat, there was A.G. in a different car, a barely three year old Ford convertible. Red and Black with red interior, dual exhausts, fender skirts, radio, top down, and ready to go. "Nice car", I said.

"Yeah, but not as nice as the Olds" was the reply. "Look here pal, I need you to go with me in the morning."

"OK, where we going?" was my answer.

"We are going to get my pole", he said. The Mississippi Power Company had presented A.G, with a bill for $87.00 for the pole he knocked down the previous night. "We are borrowing one of my old man's trucks and I am going to get my pole." This was the first I knew his Dad had trucks. "If I have to pay them for the pole, then it belongs to me, and I want my $87 pole." I could see the logic of this.

So, the next day, A.G. showed up in a truck with a trailer attached, and we drove to the Mississippi Power Company yard, which was between Meridian Avenue and 1st Avenue near the Railroad Tracks. Upon our arrival, A.G. very politely showed the man at the yard the bill for $87 marked paid and said, "We are here for this pole!"

The man was dumbfounded. "No one has ever asked for the pole," he said.

"Well," said A.G., "perhaps you would like to refund my money then!" The man went inside to talk on the phone.

In a few minutes, he came out and said, "the pole was burned as trash."

"OK then, we will just take a substitute, as long as it is equal to my pole," was A.G.'s reply. Back inside went the poor man. In a few minutes out he came with his reply.

"The pole you hit was broken, so it was burned as trash."

"No problem," said A.G. "I will accept a broken pole as long as it is equal to my pole."

Back inside the man went. This time a different man came out. "What is the problem here," he wanted to know? So, back through the same story we went. This guy seemed to be the boss and was eager to get rid of us so he offered a compromise. "What if I give y'all 10 bucks and you boys go away?"

A.G. thanked him for his offer but declined and asked, "who is the head man for Mississippi Power Company for Laurel?"

"I will be right back," the man said and went inside. About 5 minutes later out he came with a slip of paper. "You boys take this voucher to the office down town and the lady at the cashier cage will give you your $87. Now leave me alone and get the hell away from here."

As we drove off, I was amazed by all this and was quiet. A.G. was humming *Rock Around the Clock* and patting the steering wheel with his left hand when he said, "At least the old man is good for something. This was his idea."

"But what would you have done if they had produced the pole", I asked.

"Well, I guess I would have just owned a broken light pole."

THE CROSLEY

My friend Colbert was a real genius, and as geniuses are prone to be, was somewhat different! To say that he marched to a different drummer was an understatement. Colbert looked like a young Marlon Brando and talked like him, was very muscular, and poised beyond his years. We shared a passion for cars, knives, bullwhips, and weird things. There was nothing that Colbert could not fix. So, I was always prevailing on him to work on my car. He knew all the tricks to make a car go faster and stay running under my abuse.

Colbert had a great love for the Crosley Auto. For those unfamiliar with the Crosley, it was a little car that was about 30 years ahead of its time. It was made from the early 40's to about 1952 or 1953. They made pick-ups, Station Wagons, Panel Wagons, and 2 door and 4 door sedans. For a couple of years Crosley made a little sports car convertible called the Crosley Hot shot. These were very small cars in a time when other cars were huge gas-guzzlers. But at 19 cents a gallon, gas was not a big deal to most people in the 50's.

There were not very many Crosleys around and no one knew how to work on them as they had a very strange engine. In fact I never saw anyone anywhere work on a Crosley except Colbert.

One hot summer morning I went by Colbert's house and found him standing beside his Crosley with a very sad look on his face. "What's up?" I inquired.

"Aw man, my Crosley just died", he lamented.

"Well, I will help you fix it", I quickly said.

"Naw, man it's lunched itself, gone, gone. I got to have a new engine. Give me a ride to Ellisville. I know an old man down there who has three Crosleys that he uses for parts. We will buy me an engine from him."

The Crosley Auto Company had been out of business for a couple of years and parts were just not available anywhere.

When we arrived at the man's home just on the outskirts if Ellisville, we saw three Crosleys in the back yard and one little Station Wagon out front. The man who owned the place and the autos was not polite or friendly. In no uncertain terms he told us nothing he had was for sale at any price, at any time, now or in the future. We needed to get gone before he sicced the dogs on us, of which he had several mean looking cross breeds lying on the porch with him. Mumbling and grumbling we got back in the car.

On the way back to Laurel I had to listen to Colbert cuss the old man and lament his bad luck. "The only Crosley's available and an old fool owns them." I dropped him off at his house, as I had to go to work at the Frosty Treat at noon and could not be late for work.

About 9 P.M. Colbert and another guy I knew came by the Frosty Treat and said "Wish us luck, we are going to the Moonlight Auto Parts Store." Which I knew was slang for going to get something that belonged to someone else; i.e. stealing. When I got off work that night I went home with no delay as I did not want to be around if there was going to be any problem with the law. Next day I stopped by Colbert's house and sure enough in the back yard was his car with the hood off and the motor lying on the ground. Under a tarp was another engine. "How did you get the motor out and across that fence?" I asked. Colbert just smiled and flexed his muscles in his right arm. "I know you are strong," I said, "but that sounds like too much."

"Well", he said, "Night and dogs add to your strength and a Crosley engine only weighs about 65 0r 70 pounds so I unbolted it and threw it over the fence. Then Al helped me get it in the car. Al hurt his back and won't help me anymore. How 'bout giving me a hand?" I begged off saying I had some errands to run before work. So I took my leave.

Several days later a friend stopped by and said "didja hear that Colbert got busted for stealing a Crosley engine?"

"No," I said in pretend shock. "What happened?" "

Well, he stole a Crosley engine in Ellisville and the owner described him and the cops went straight to Colbert's house and there he was working on the car. So, they arrested him and hc is out on bond right now."

The next day I stopped by Colbert's house to see him and he was somewhat subdued. "Yeah, man John Friendly got me." John Friendly was our term for the law.

"What you gonna do?" I wondered aloud.

"Well, right now I got to see Judge Montgomery and see what he says. How 'bout riding me up town?"

So we went to town to see the Judge. I decided to go along for moral support. The Judge was very stern and proceeded to lecture Colbert about the perils of a life of crime. The upshot was that Colbert was subject to go to prison for several years or maybe probation, pending good behavior with close supervision of probation and any misstep would land him in prison. But the Judge said he needed to think about it so "come back in three days" for his decision.

As we somberly walked out of the Judge's office onto the street a Marine Corps Recruiter accosted us. He was as pretty as a picture, creases so sharp you could shave on them, shirt absolutely fitted like a second skin, necktie straight as a plumb line, cap exactly over his eyebrows, narrow waist, flat stomach, erect as a telephone pole, and a swagger stick under his arm. With a click of his heels he stopped and tapped Colbert on the shoulder with the swagger stick. "Let me talk to you boys about the Marine Corps," he said with obvious pride.

We stopped, and Colbert looked him up and down and said very politely "Sir, my next several years have just been spoken for."

TUFFY

Working at the Frosty Treat in Laurel Mississippi as a teenager was a great job. Everyone in Laurel came by at least once a day. The parking lot was circular and I could see everyone as they drove by on South Magnolia or came to eat or just park and visit. I worked from twelve noon until closing time in the summers and after school and weekends when school was in. I would work about sixty or seventy hours a week in the summertime for the forty bucks a week I was paid. Every Saturday night was payday and time to party, party, party. I was very happy with my job and pay.

The people that owned the place treated me like family and were great folks to work for. When I got to work at noon I could grab a cheeseburger off the grill, a piece of fried chicken, or just about anything I chose to eat or drink.

At closing time my job was to clean up and disinfect the ice cream machines. We had two big chrome Mills machines that were a chore to clean so I seldom got out before 11:00 or 11:30 and sometimes midnight. When I got off I always had some friends waiting to go somewhere.

The social aspects alone were worth more than the forty dollars a week I made. I met most of my running mates while working at the Frosty Treat, and when I got off I would join them in our favorite pastime of riding from Drive In to Drive

In from service station to service station looking for other people like ourselves (late-nighters) and looking for girls to talk to. But nice girls were not out at this time of night, and the ones who were out had dates.

Working at the Frosty Treat was perfect for girl looking. Many would just ride by and wave. But some would stop and have something to eat and visit. My being inside did not hinder me from flirting with every girl who came on the place, date or no date.

One girl would always give me a big smile and wave if her date were not looking. When he would get out of the car to place their order she would smile and behind his back would flirt with me the whole time they were there. Her boyfriend drove a beautiful yellow Packard Convertible only a couple of years old. He was from the Gulf Coast and his family had a large seafood packing company. He came to Laurel to see her on weekends. He was a very tall young man, probably about six feet four or five. He was a well-built handsome guy but he frowned all the time and was not friendly at all. So, I went out of my way to flirt with this girl when they came by, which was usually Saturday night.

One Saturday night after I got off about Midnight I was riding with several of my buddies and we met the big yellow convertible. The boyfriend had several of his friends with him. As we passed he gave us the old one finger salute, whereupon I responded with the same salute. After making the block and heading uptown we met the yellow Packard again. I had three buddies in my car and they all yelled and gestured. The Packard responded in kind. About ten minutes later our paths crossed again on Ellisville Boulevard. This time the driver motioned for us to follow. Quick to accept a challenge we followed them to behind Breland's Fruit Stand where the street connected with the Goodyear's parking lot.

As we pulled up beside the Packard, the driver said "get out smart aleck, I am going to beat your ass." Being somewhat cocky and not wanting to appear cowardly to my friends, I jumped out and ran toward him. We stood toe to toe and punched each other in the face. It was a short, brutal fight. Every blow was in the face or head. After about 10 or 12 blows we both, as if on a signal dropped our arms and stared at each other. Both of us were bleeding. We both had bloody noses, split lips, cuts on cheekbones and swollen eyes. I knew I would have a black eye tomorrow and would look like hell. Without a word, he turned and got in his car and they drove off.

My buddy's all began to brag on me. "Boy, you showed his big ass." however I felt like I had been run over by a big truck. My right eye was rapidly swelling shut, and blood was dripping down my chin. My right ear was burning and felt as thick as a phone book. I was a wreck!

We drove down to Seal's Service Station to wash up and to try to clean some blood from my clothes. My pals were still bragging on my "winning" the fight. As I was in the restroom washing my face with my handkerchief and trying to look presentable, I heard some loud talking and looked out the door. The Packard had driven up in front of the restroom door and the driver was getting out. My friend Gerald, who was about 5 feet 6 and maybe 140 pounds, was jawing and with him. "Okay, Tuffy, you want some more of this? We are ready to give you all you want." This was when I learned that his nickname was Tuffy. In a flash I grabbed Gerald by the shirt and said in a whisper, "Hell no, he don't want any more. He has had all I can stand."

MIKE THE KNIFE

Years before the great Bobby Darren had a hit song entitled
"Mack The Knife" Laurel Mississippi had a citizen that we all
knew as" Mike The Knife." Mike had this nickname because
of his having cut several people in fights around the Laurel
area. Mike was a slim, good looking guy about six feet tall,
very neat and clean. He smiled a lot but was famous for
having a very quick temper.

He worked at the Masonite plant in Laurel, with at that time
about 3,000 other guys. This was a big factory! Masonite made
the world famous Masonite board and ran three shifts of eight
hours each, round the clock 7 days a week, 365 days a year.
Mike worked the 7am to 3pm shift so was always around the
night spots and places we frequented after dark. People that
worked at the Masonite plant in certain jobs were issued a
Hawk Billed knife to mark the boards. These were very good
knives with a big hooked blade about four inches long that
folded into the wooden handle. When very sharp this was a
serious weapon and very intimidating, Mike could get his
knife out of his back pocket and open it faster than any one I
had ever seen! It was just a blur and then snap, it was open
and ready to do whatever.

I always got along with Mike, mostly because he considered
us kin folks. His last name was a very common one in Jones
County and he considered us kin because my great
grandmother had married a guy who was a widower with

three children. They had four children together then he died, after which my great grandmother married his brother, who was also a widower with four children and they had five children together, so here was one family with 16 children all with the same last name and bloodlines and same mother or father. Mike was descended from the family of husband number one so we were third cousins or something like that and Mike considered us kin folks, much to my relief, because whenever a fight would start I was always on the good side of Mike and his knife.

One summer night in 1954 just after dark, we were hanging out at a popular drive inn establishment talking and wishing some girls would come by, when a big new sporty Pontiac convertible drove up. Two guys we did not know got out and went to the window to order some food. These guys were dressed in all western attire, cowboy hats, fancy shirts, jeans and fancy cowboy boots. As we all wore white tee shirts, jeans and penny loafers, these two fellows looked way out of place, so Mike walked over to them and said "Well Howdy podners. Are you Cowboys looking for directions to the Ranch"?

We all laughed and giggled at this. One of the cowboys looked Mike up and down and retorted, "If I was, I would ask your daddy, little boy!! Or do you know who your daddy is?" Wow. This was a real insult, and a challenge of the Nth degree. It got real quiet for a second, then like a flash out came the famous knife, just as quick, a fat snub nosed revolver appeared in the cowboys hand!

The sound of that revolver cocking was one of the loudest noises I can remember, the cowboy said "take one step back sonny boy or your friends will pick you up." We all backed up at once. The second cowboy walked over with his gun in hand and said "We are leaving with our food and anyone who tries to stop us or follow us will learn why you do not take a knife to a gun fight!!"

We never saw or heard about these two cowboys after this affair, and I do not remember Mike ever cutting anyone after this or even pulling his knife in anger.

THE TOUGHEST GUY I EVER KNEW

As a teenager I ran around with a diverse group of guys. I was always the youngest one in the group, except in rare cases when I had my younger brother Stuart with me, for some reason or the other. Stuart, even though nearly two years younger than I, was big for his age and very strong and had a mean streak about a yard wide, so he fit in alright when he was with us. The other guys quickly learned not to mess with Stuart because he and I made a formidable team and we always looked out for each other. At any sign of trouble we would be side by side or back to back for the duration of the problem.

Several guys in our group had dropped out of high school and were working in the oil fields or at one of the factories in the area. These guys, due to working shift work, would be around for a week or so then their shift would change from day to night shift and we would not see them for a week or so. Ben was one of the guys who worked on a drilling rig in the oil fields. Ben would be around when he was not on the drilling rig. He would usually show up at night when we were at some drive in, or a night spot or at the Pan Am Service Station and Tire Recapping facility at the 5 points intersection in Laurel Mississippi. This place stayed open all night 7 days a week, and tires being the problem they were in the 1950,s was always a busy place, so naturally we hung out there, knowing some of our group would show up usually about 10:30 or 11 pm.

We would park on the spacious parking lot, go in and buy cokes and cigarettes and sit on the hoods and fenders of our cars and talk and listen to the radios. Ben usually was an early arrival as he had never been known to have a date or even have a girlfriend. Ben would get off work on the drilling rig, get cleaned up, and show up where ever we were wearing his usual cheerful grin

Ben was very stocky, bordering on fat, stood about 5 feet 8 inches tall, broad shoulders thick chest, huge biceps very big thick hands which never seemed to be completely clean due to years of working on the rigs. Grease and crude oil just seemed to penetrate the pores of the skin on his hands.

Ben was famous for his upper body strength. Once on a bet he picked up the rear end of a Studebaker truck, clearing both wheels off the pavement, only for a second, but enough to win the bet. Studebaker trucks were not the heaviest trucks on the market but I never knew anyone to duplicate this feat. Ben had the reputation of being one of the truly tough guys of our part of the world. One reason being an event that I witnessed one night.

Ben was having brake problems on his old Chevrolet 4 door sedan, so he jacked up the left rear side and removed the wheel to gain access to the brake drum and wheel cylinder. After removing the brake drum, Ben discovered a leak at the wheel cylinder. To fix this problem Ben needed more room to work, so after the jack was at the max height, Ben got the old standby auto repair helper, a Coke case, stood it on end. Under the axle makes a perfect stand, strong and steady, however it needs to be on level ground which this parking lot was not! In a few minutes the repair job was done "by plugging the brake line at the wheel cylinder with a nail". Three wheel brakes are nearly as good as four wheel brakes, if you are careful. When getting ready to let the jack down, Ben reached to get the Coke case from under the axle, at that moment the jack shifted, and the car fell off the old bumper jack, trapping Ben's right hand between the Coke case and the axle. The full weight of the car was not on Ben's hand due to the tire being trapped in the wheel well by Bens left shoulder, but it was a serious situation and Ben was in a very awkward and painful position.

With a loud grunt, and a deep breath, Ben said in a kinda normal tone of voice, "Y'all need to pick this car up off of me now." Four or five of us jumped in to help. Ben directed four of us to grab the rear bumper and one to reset the jack. 1-2-3 go and we all lifted and someone reset the jack and Ben was free. Ben walked around in circles for few minutes holding his hand. We tried to get him to go to the Laurel General Hospital which was only about 100 yards west of us at the top of the 5 points intersection, but Ben was afraid they would put his hand in a cast or wrap it up and cause him to miss work, so we packed his hand in ice and sure enough in about an hour,

Ben announced that he was ok, and ready for whatever we could find to do, sore hand and all.

The one thing that defined Ben as the toughest guy I ever saw happened several weeks later. On a Saturday night we were all hanging out at the Pan Am Service station standing around talking when a very nice, brand new Buick pulled up to the station. Two guys we had never seen got out and went inside, we wandered over to admire the shiny Buick. Ben was standing near the driver's side door when the two strangers came out. The driver brushed by Ben to open the door and loudly said "watch it fatso, you are too close to my car."

Ben quickly asked "who you calling fatso? You jerk!!" In a flash the stranger closed the door and punched Ben in the face. Ben only shook his head and squared off at the stranger. Seeing that his blow had not fazed Ben the stranger whipped out a knife from his belt and cut Ben across the waistline from right to left. Suddenly blood was dripping through Bens fingers as he held his stomach with both hands. Ben backed up, looked down at his bleeding waist, then looked at the stranger and said in a loud voice "I will get you for this you so and so and I will get you good."

"Hey," said the stranger, "you are going the wrong way, I am over here fatso, you need to come this way to get me."

In a very calm voice Ben said "Right now I got to hunt me up a doctor. But when I find me a Doctor, and he sews me up I will be after you like white on rice!! Just wait right here, the hospital is just up the street and I will be right back!!

Ben started walking towards the hospital. We all rushed to help him and we heard the Buick crank up and drive off the other direction. We never saw the two guys or the Buick again, though Ben was always on the lookout for them, and Ben only missed two days work and had a nifty scar across his middle.

I LOVE OLD FORDS

Old Fords hold a special place in my heart. Even today at my advanced age I can walk around one, open the door, and the very distinct smell brings a flood of memories. It is a visceral thing, so strong I can nearly taste it.

Nothing smells like an old Ford; nothing feels or drives like an old Ford; nothing sounds like an old Ford, from the erratic bumpy idle of the "T" model or an "A" model to the low snarl of a Flathead Ford V8.

The Flathead Ford V8 became the early Hot Rod delight when Ford introduced the V8 in 1932 and after World War II. When making cars go faster became a national craze, the Flathead Ford V8 was the weapon of choice. The Flathead V8 was available everywhere, cheap and very easy to work on. Anyone with a few simple tools could make a Ford V8 run and run fast, and best of all, stay running.

The very day I turned 15 years old my father handed me the keys to a 1941 Ford 2-door sedan, army green in color and said, "Let's go get you a driver's license." (I had been driving for about a year.) We went to Laurel and in two hours flat I was a legal driver and the new errand boy for the McBride household: Mother to work, my Granny to the drugstore and beauty shop, my younger sister to ballet lessons, my brother to wherever he could think of and my older sister to piano lessons and social events. Although my sister was two years older than I, and a wonderful musician, she could never cope with a cranky old stick shift Ford so I ran the roads every day, happy to be going hither and yon just as long as I could drive. Nothing made me happier than to learn that I had multiple errands and a real schedule to follow.

In between runs and trips I would aimlessly ride looking for new territory and if no one was with me, a new challenge, such as a long sweeping curve on a gravel road, the rear wheel hanging out close to the ditch, controlling the slide with the gas pedal, gently getting on and off the gas to come out of the curve going straight ahead full blast, wheels spinning, gravel flying, motor screaming. It was one of the great joys of youth.

Quickly I learned the limitations of the ugly old '41 Ford and with a little help from my friends, installed a dual exhaust system with "Smithy" mufflers. Pronounced "Smitty" but spelled "Smithy." These mufflers were alleged to increase horsepower and gas mileage but I suspect only served to increase the sound level by many decibels, and encouraged me to run faster and to leave the old Ford in second gear longer to get the sweet sound of the dual exhaust rumbling behind me. New hot sparkplugs, bigger jets in the carb, and dual points in the distributor all helped to make the ugly old sedan run much better and a lot faster.

Just about the time I got the old thing running to my satisfaction I totally destroyed it (and nearly myself) in a horrific wreck which left me in the hospital and the car in the junkyard.

While I was in the hospital my ever patient father bought a 1942 Ford coupe with a later model Mercury engine in it. (Years later I learned that 1942 autos were very rare due to the second World War ending production for civilian markets in early '42.)

After getting out of the hospital and healing up somewhat, I gleefully went back to my running the roads day and night. The old 1942 coupe was a teenager's dream - jet black with lots of chrome, spotlight on the driver's side, sleek and fast, radio that worked most of the time, the light body and shorter wheelbase of the coupe made it a joy to drive. It was quick and agile and already had a "Smithy" muffler with the addition of a chrome tailpipe extension. I was ready to go.

Tires were always a problem in those days, what with me feeling the absolute necessity of spinning the tires on every departure (that is if my parents were not in earshot or view) and sliding sideways through every curve in Jones County and standing up on the brakes to make a quicker stop and to hear the tires slide. The usual remedy for slick, flat, or blown-out tires was to go to the Pan Am service station and tire recapping facility between the underpass and five-points intersection in Laurel. The Pan Am stayed open all night, and you could limp in with a flat or blow-out and have a tire recapped for $3.00 if you would wait an hour or more, or you could purchase a fresh recap from inventory for $6.00 and be on your way in a few minutes. The $6.00 recapped tire looked brand new and was guaranteed to get you out of sight. With my driving tactics, I became a regular customer, and if I did not have any money, the owner would let me sign a ticket until the next day, because he knew my father, and knew he would get the money.

Changing a flat tire was a fact of life in those days, and we prided ourselves on the speed of our tire-changing skills. Most weekends included at least one flat tire and a side-of-the-road tire change. The problem was that most flat tires were at inconvenient times and places. If you were running late to get your date home by a specific time (and all nice girls had a curfew), you could be assured of having a flat, and usually in busy traffic. While you got all greasy and dirty, your date would remind you of the time and that her father did not really like you anyhow, so you'd best hurry! When you arrived at your date's home, she would be in a rush to get inside so you, being all nasty with dirty hands, would get no goodnight kiss.

So back downtown to get cleaned up and have the flat fixed if at all possible, because riding around with no spare tire was tempting fate to such a degree as to be just plain foolhardy. Plus, you could always depend on several of your buddies being at the Pan Am with the same problem, or just waiting around, knowing that some of our group would show up about 11 0'clock or so. Anyone who did not have a date could depend on finding some of us there by this time of night. Then we would gang up in one or two cars and enjoy our favorite pastime of riding aimlessly from place to place, radio blaring WLAC, Randy's Record Shop: WLAC always the station of choice this time of night.

After a year of my driving the '42 coupe as fast as it would go everywhere I went, the motor was getting very tired, and I was putting a quart of oil in every day, sometimes two quarts a day just to get around. One spring day, facing major repairs on my car, my father in a moment of weakness let me talk him into trading it for a beautiful 1950 Ford 4-door sedan, light green, clean as a pin, good radio and heater, whitewall tires, a fresh overhauled V8 with a new clutch. I was in heaven. This was a nice car!! After cautioning me to drive very carefully, he handed me the keys. With a fervent promise to be the very soul of decorum and thanking him profusely, I drove off.

The very moment he was out of sight, I popped second gear and floored the gas. With tires screaming, I headed out Highway 15 South to about six miles south to Tucker's Crossing where the highway was absolutely flat and straight for about two miles crossing the Boguehoma Creek swamps. This area was a favorite place to race, and everyone knew where the "Flats" were. My joy was unbounded when I found that the '50 Ford would indicate 100 miles per hour, and if I held it down would slowly creep past the 100 mph mark and would hang straight down, smooth and without vibration and rattle usually found in old cars at these speeds. I was one happy teenager.

This car carried me through the summer and all through my senior year of high school and would still run nearly 100 mph after taking a year of my daily abuse.

Of the many, many autos (too many to count) I have owned in my life, the 1950 Ford V8 is my all-time favorite and I wish I had it now.

ROCK AND ROLL

I have always loved music. Many of my early and fond memories are of my sister Jean, [the greatest piano player in the universe], playing in our living room. I could be across the road playing cops and robbers, or cowboys and Indians I could hear the beautiful sounds of the piano coming out of the open windows and doors of our house. (No air conditioning)

I would hum along with this beautiful music, and the sounds were perfect in my head, but I learned to my dismay that I could not sing or whistle a tune. Everyone in my family could sing, play, hum, and whistle. But alas, I could only listen to the beautiful music. I tried to learn to sing, but no recognizable sound came out. So, I would just sing to myself.

When someone would hit a wrong note singing or playing, I would cringe. A wrong note was like fingernails on a blackboard to me. Music was a joy to me and I loved to hear my sister practicing for hours on end. My brain just soaked up the music, by the time I was about 12 or 13 I could recognize most of the classics.

In my teen years we listened to the radio all the time. When just riding around aimlessly, the radio was always on. The local stations signed off about 10:30PM or thereabouts, and then we could get the real stations; WLAC Nashville, WLS Chicago, KAAY Little Rock, KWKH Shreveport, LA, and the best of all, XERF the voice of Del Rio, Texas. XERF was really in Mexico. It was so powerful that they had to move into Mexico, nine miles South of the border into Via Acunia but they continued to broadcast as Del Rio, Texas.

Rock and Roll was just coming into power. The local stations would not play any music that hinted of Rock, so after the nice folks were in bed; we teenagers began to twirl the dials in our cars and trucks to find these stations, as we rode aimlessly about as teenagers always have done looking for something to do.

These were 50,000-Watt Clear Channel AM Stations, and on a good night, we could pick up all of them. WLAC was a pioneer in the playing of Rock Music. By about 1953 they were playing Little Richard, Joe Turner, and Ivory Joe Hunter. No local stations in our part of the world would play any black music. So, until 10 or so, we had to listen to Kay Starr (who I really liked), Jo Stafford, Kitty Kallen, Etc. About 11 P.M .WLAC's Randy's Record Shop with Gene Nobles came on the air blasting all over the central states with the music we were waiting for. All Rock, mostly black performers. Chuck Berry with his rendition of Maybelline caught the soul of teen-age boys all over the Country. The more parents, teachers, clergy and figures of authority ranted and raved against Rock and Roll, the more we wanted to hear.

The movie "Blackboard Jungle" was the first real teen movie. They borrowed Bill Haley's Rock Around the Clock as the theme song. I guess I saw that weak movie at least 6 times.

But in July of 1954 the real deal burst upon the scene Uninvited and Unannounced, Elvis Presley with "That's Alright Momma" and "Blue Moon of Kentucky". Elvis hit like a tornado. Every parent's worst nightmare. A wild eyed, twisting, gyrating, Royal Crown Pomaded menace to all right thinking, God-fearing folks. Dewey Phillips, DJ on WDIA Memphis Red Hot and Blue Show, played "That's Alright Momma" 30 times the day he got it and the phones lines lit up each time, As callers begged for more.

In Boston, Massachusetts, the Reverend John Carroll told the Archdiocese that "Rock and Roll inflames and excites youth like the Jungle Tom Toms readying the warriors for battle." The reference to Tom Toms was not out of the same book as "Love thy Neighbor as Thy Self" because everyone knew who beat Tom Toms.

Rock and Roll caused one of the first cracks or fissures of what would be later known as the "Generation Gap" .As what we thought of as "our music" came under attack by the establishment, we became protective and possessive. Critics in the media and churches became more active and vocal and went to extreme lengths to denigrate any and all who listened to Rock and Roll.

The First Baptist Church of Laurel, Mississippi held a public burning of Rock and Roll Records and Music. They made a huge bonfire in the middle of the street and people were invited to pile all their records and music on the fire, especially Elvis Presley who was looked upon as the Anti-Christ by most preachers. This little Fahrenheight 451 became a rallying point for us Rockers and steeled our will to listen to ROCK !

Everyone was buying portable radios. The industry reported that in 1953 they sold over 3 million. This gave us the power to listen to what we wanted to. When we wanted to.

We would gather late at night and listen to WLAC's Late Nite Show with the DJ touting "Royal Crown Pomade." From midnight until about 3 A.M. we could listen to shake Rattle and Roll, Corrina Corrina, Since You Left Me Baby, and Maybelline.

My friend, Colbert, made a 45 RPM record player that fit under the dash of a car and would slide out and you could choose your own song, and not be at the mercy of the DJ. However, the needle scratched the record if the car was moving on anything but a very smooth street, of which Laurel Mississippi had very few. My buddy A.G. bought this device from Colbert and installed it under the dash of his Ford convertible which was a huge success. When parked, you could slide it out and play the records you chose.

One night I was sitting at Nub's Drive Inn listening the Juke Box, which was outside in a little house with speakers, wondering where all by buddies were when a person I did not know came up to my car, directed by one of the carhops, both of which I knew very well. "I have a message for you. A man on the Ridge Road named A.G. flagged me down and asked if I would tell you that he is stranded up there, for you to come and get him. He said bring jumper cables." After directions, I headed out. We never went anywhere without jumper cables anyhow!

Arriving at A.G. and his disabled car I discovered that he and his date had been parked at a romantic spot overlooking the valley where Laurel sits listening to the 45-RPM record player that Colbert had sold him and installed in his Ford Convertible. It seems that about 18 minutes without the motor running was all it took to run the battery completely down. A.G. was very angry about the deal, as was the girl, who was about 2 hours late in getting home. After getting him cranked, A.G. roared off to get the girl home, and to try to fade the heat.

I rode back to Nubs parking lot and in a few minutes Colbert came up and I began to tell the story of A.G. and the record player deal. Colbert began to laugh and said, "I guess he did not believe me when I told him to do whatever he was going to in about 5 songs if the motor was not running." (45-RPM Records last about 2 to3 minutes each.)

THE BOUNCER

For many years I was prone to frequent roadside taverns, also called honky tonks, or juke joints. Very few were upscale enough to be referred to as a "Bar".

The Laurel-Hattiesburg area was richly endowed with these places. Every highway had several of these interesting places just outside of Town. This was prior to legal drinking and liquor stores. You could always count on one of these places being open for business day or night on every route in this part of Mississippi.

On a cold and rainy winter night I was headed back to Laurel, Mississippi from Meridian, and just South of Sandersville, Mississippi, I saw the lights of the "Old Confederate Inn". This establishment was once a skating rink and had been converted into the "The Old Confederate Inn", a true den of iniquity. Seeing the auto of a friend on the gravel parking lot, I decided to stop and have a beer. Upon entering the cavernous building, I found my friend sitting at the bar and talking to the owner who I knew from way back. The inside of the building was as warm and toasty, as it was empty. Only my friend and the proprietor were in the huge building that was lighted by the warm glow of a jukebox and some beer sign with several gas heaters giving cheery warmth.

A few minutes later in walked a guy that I knew from the area. This guy was an ex-football player at Southern Mississippi and had played some professional football. He was a large young man with a very bad attitude and a famous short fuse. I nodded and said "Hi, give everyone a beer on me." which ensured peace, at least for a while, as the jukebox kept a soft nasal refrain in the background. We talked in vague generalities for a few minutes.

Then, in walked a very short, stocky young man with a cheerful, round face on his very round head, which seemed to be sitting on his shoulders with no trace of a neck. Muddy boots and coveralls were his attire, which made him look like a green fireplug. With a happy "hi y'all, gimme a Budweiser," he walked up to the bar and, uninvited, began to join in the conversation. "Man, how nice and warm in here" he said. "This is the right place for me I been on a drilling rig for 10 hours and am about froze to death. I need me a inside job like in here. Do you need any help around here?" he addressed the owner with a cheerful grin.

"Naw, I don't guess so" was the answer. I was getting nervous because I could see the football player frowning and becoming very tense, with muscles standing out in his thick neck and jaws grinding. "What kind of work do you think you could do, fatso?" he asked with a sneer.

I began to get my feet under me for a dash for the door; because I knew it was going to get bad very soon. My friend looked at me with a puzzled look as if he had no idea what was going on. I very subtly shook my head in a "no" motion to let him know to shut up and not get involved.

The young, stocky lad, still with a grin said, "Oh, I thought maybe I could be the bouncer and keep order in here."

"I Am the Bouncer Here, Fatso" said the football player, "and I don't need no help from a fat hick!"

"Well, if I whipped your ass and threw you out would that make me the bouncer?" was the instant retort. Before any of us could move or speak the football player rushed towards the stocky lad. The young man hit the football player about 6 or 7 times right in the face so fast I could not follow the blows. It was like a piston it was so fast, just a blur and a "splat, splat, splat." Then in a movement so quick we could not believe he grabbed the big man by his collar and flung him out the door into the muddy gravel and kicked him in his backside as he went by. With a nonchalant easy move, he turned to the owner and said "Well Now! Does that make me the bouncer here? "

The owner had the presence of mind to say "Damn right, son, welcome to the Old Confederate Inn."

THE RACE CAR

I have always been obsessed with cars. As a child 8 years old I could tell the make and model of any car passing by. I remember the Tucker Torpedo on the cover of a slick paper magazine (Probably Life) when I was about 10 years old and I thought it was the most beautiful thing I had ever seen.

In the early fifty's the Indy cars were the ultimate in speed and beauty. The roadsters graceful curves and perfect proportions defined speed and power to a young boy. We could only dream of seeing an Indy car in our small town world.

My hometown, Laurel, Mississippi, was a hot bed of fast cars. Laurel had a half-mile oval dirt tract with a covered grandstand, which seated several hundred people. The races were well attended and everyone had a favorite driver and car. The races were held at the South Mississippi Fairgrounds just south of downtown Laurel on Ellisville Blvd. Many Saturday nights my parents would let me walk with my buddies the several miles to the fairgrounds to see the car races. People came from several states to race at the Laurel racetrack, Donnie and Bobby Allison, and Red Farmer from Alabama were regulars at the Laurel track.

After I had moved away from Laurel, I would still on occasion come back to see the Saturday night races. When I moved back to Laurel in the Mid-Sixties, I discovered to my delight that the track was still in use and had been paved to make a racers dream. A ½ mile asphalt oval, I could not stand it until I had a race car of my own. With the help of my brother-in-law (a real mechanic) we built a race car out of an old 1940 Ford coupe and began to race.

But every week, looking at the sleek sprint cars evoking memories of Indy type cars, I began to want a pro-type sprinter. Someone told me of a real well built racer sitting in a garage near Laurel gathering dust. Getting directions to the garage, my brother-in-law and I set out to purchase this car. The car was alleged to be at Beat Four, Mississippi which shows on the map as Whistler, Mississippi. But everyone knew it as Beat Four on Highway 84 East in Wayne County. We began to ask, and were given directions to Tyners Garage a little ways out in the country. Arriving at a fork in the road we saw a tin building with a sign saying Tyners garage. Going inside we were greeted by a slim, older man, (maybe 60) but old to our 20 something years, dressed in Khaki work clothes, grease stained with a wrench in his hand.

"Are you Mr. Tyner" I asked.

"Yep", he replied. "What can I do for you?"

As my eyes adjusted to the dim light in the building, I saw behind him, in the center of the garage up on stands, a beautiful burgundy colored sprint car. Chrome wheels, chrome headers, old dropped style axle, quick change rear end, small block Chevy engine, tall stack Hilborn Injectors, a racers dream come true; as well built a car as I could dream of. "Mr. Tyner", I repeated.

"Yep" he said. "What can I do for you?" with a touch of impatience in his voice.

"We want to look at your car" I managed to mumble.

His demeanor changed at once. His shoulders became square and erect. With a hint of a smile He said "there she is." Ain't she's a beaut?" My brother-in-law was practically drooling as we walked around the car as it sat in state in the center of the shop, not a speck of dust, not a scratch, not a speck of rust even on the exhaust side of the motor, not a drop of oil.

"Will she run", I asked very quietly.

"Will she run" he laughed. "As good as the day she last won a race at Jackson, Mississippi Speedway. I crank her up every once in a great while" he said somewhat wistfully, "and sometimes run her down the road when no one is around."

"Mr. Tyner, would you consider selling her to me?" I asked very humbly.

"Son, she is not for sale at any price. Many people have tried to buy her, but there ain't no way or conditions that I would ever sell her."

"But Mr. Tyner, don't you want to see her race again?" I said.

"Son, she will never race again", he said very firmly.

"Why don't you race her at Laurel?" I asked.

"Son, she nor I will ever be at a track again."

"But why not?" I asked.

"Son, I become a Christian!"

"What has that to do with racing?" I asked.

"Son, where ever they's fast cars, they's fast women and fast money, you know that? You cain't be a Christian and race cars. It's been nice talking to you boys, but I have work to do. Stop in and see me if you get back this way again." And with that he turned his back on us and picked up his tools. Knowing we had been dismissed, we eased out and got in the car to go back to Laurel.

With a wistful backward look, we headed out. We were very quiet for a few miles. Then somewhat under my breath, I said, "where ever they's fast cars, they's fast women, and fast money". "I sure hope that's true", my brother-in-law said.

MY FRIEND BUBBY

In my high school years (early 50's) it was not uncommon for a guy to drop out of school and get a job or go into the armed forces, usually about the 10th grade or age 17 which ever came first. Many of these guys, especially if they were big and strong would go to work in the oil fields. Laurel Mississippi was the center of the oil drilling industry in the deep south.

Several large drilling companies operated out of Laurel, plus several trucking companies that specialized in moving drilling rigs from location to location, which was a big undertaking. Many trucks and lots of strong men were needed to move a drilling rig. And it was usually moved to a remote area deep in the piney woods away from any roads.

So now a road had to be built all the way in to the location, usually this was a board road made from rough cut oak timbers 8x8 and 6x6 on the sides then 4x8 laid across them.

This made a very sturdy road, but very labor intensive, which made for many job opportunities, for young guys with strong backs and the will to work in all kinds of conditions and to make above average pay.

Bubby was slow talking, slow walking, good looking guy with a pretty good head on his shoulders and a very good work ethic. After leaving school at the end of the 10th grade at about the age of 18 or so, he set out to make his way in the world. The oil fields seemed the fastest way to make good money and stay in the Laurel area.

Bubby was so named by his sisters, he was the only boy and had 3 older sisters one of whom called him Bubby instead of brother. The name stuck and thereafter he was known as Bubby. I do not remember anyone ever calling him by his given name.

With a good work ethic and a cheerful attitude Bubby quickly advanced to foreman on a board road building crew, then got on as a roustabout (a helper on a drilling rig) then was promoted to a roughneck, which was a high paying job for that time.

After several years Bubby was promoted to Driller, a real serious, high paying job in the industry. All this time Bubby had been dating the same girl, the daughter of a very wealthy man in our area, this girl was so in love with Bubby that nothing would do but for them to marry. The girl's family was not pleased at her plans to marry a greasy, oil soaked 10th grade dropout, but true love prevailed and they got married in a real big, high society wedding. Bubby got cleaned up and degreased, even wore a tux with a tie.

After the happy couple got back from the honeymoon the father of the bride called Bubby into his office and informed him that a worker on a drilling rig was not a fit husband for his daughter so he had bought (sight unseen) a used drilling rig in west Texas and was having it delivered to Laurel Mississippi for Bubby to start drilling operations. Bubby would now be a big time oil operator, not just a Roughneck in greasy overalls.

In the oil drilling business wells are drilled by major oil companies. These companies have teams of geologists and engineers who do all kinds of seismic studies to find where to drill and how deep. The ratio of drilling a successful oil well to drilling a dry hole is about 8 or 9 dry holes (failure to produce) to every producing well. Bubby as a wildcat driller had no geologists or engineers or any one qualified to figure out where to drill or how deep so Bubby leased some passed over land just north and east of Laurel in Clarke County. After the usual delays in getting the rig renovated, updated and moved to the location, and hiring all his old cronies as a crew, Bubby started to drill for oil.

Naturally Bubby hits a very good producing well on his first try. Money starts flowing, other people want to invest, so Bubby tries again, another producing well, and another, and another, 8 producing wells in a row, no dry holes, this is unheard of in the business.

Bubby is now a real live genius, money, money, money, flowing like one of Bubby's best wells. Father In law is now very proud of his daughter's choice of a mate. Bubby now builds a great big house, buys several big cars,(Bubby loved Buicks) takes up smoking big fat cigars and drinking Crown Royal instead of Early Times all day and most of the night.

On one of his late night excursions Bubby was in a brand new Buick Electra 225 and was going across town to replenish his stock of Crown Royal whiskey. This was before legal liquor in Mississippi, so places that sold whiskey were always just outside of town, in the county. The GM&O railroad runs right through the middle of Laurel from the north to the south, RR crossings were all plainly marked. Some had flashing lights, loud bells, and big signs etc. Well, it was late, Bubby was in a hurry and quite possibly somewhat impaired, when he turned left from Ellisville Blvd. to cross the tracks.

A train was passing by, at whatever speed trains have to go when passing through a town at night, Bubby never saw the train and center punched it about halfway between the locomotive and the caboose. The impact knocked Bubby's Buick down the tracks and rolled it over several times. The car was a smoking ruin and Bubby was transported to the local hospital with a badly cut head, several broken bones, and many cuts and bruises, after several days in the hospital Bubby went home to recuperate.

Several days later a claims adjuster and two lawyers from the GM&O RR came by Bubby's home to try to settle with him. Railroads always tried to settle out of court in those days because they knew that Jury trials always went bad for the RR Co and they hoped to settle on the spot with as little hoorah as possible. So with checkbook in hand they came to see Bubby. He was in his bedroom all propped up in bed and bandaged all over. It being about 11 a.m. Bubby had had only a few shots of Crown Royal and was in pretty good form. His wife had told him who the men were, so Bubby was waiting, loaded for bear. Before they could say a word Bubby blurts out, "Look here, I am sorry about your D**** ole train. I was drunk and I did not see it so I will just pay for any damage I done to it, OK??"

"Oh, just sign this release" they said, "and we will just forget all about this matter."

Bubby signed, and they got out at once.

MORE ABOUT BUBBY

After Bubby had the encounter with the train in his brand new Buick Electra 225 (which was a disaster for the 225 and Bubby's head), Bubby seemed to undergo a personality change. I believe the head injury was far worse than we all thought at the time because after healing up some he no longer had the drive to work all day. He would not get up till about 10 am or so, which was not like him at all. His consumption of Crown Royal doubled, he started drinking upon arising and did not stop till he went to sleep, at whatever late hour that was.

Before the advent of legal liquor stores and bars in our fine state the Holiday Inn just outside of Laurel on Highway 11 North had a fine bar. The owner of the place (an uncle of mine) had the premises (8 acres) declared a legal resort area. This took some legal conniving and strange doings and wining and dining some legislators, but finally worked out ok.

So now the Holiday Inn had the right to sell alcohol on premises to the public. You could get a drink with your meal in the dining room, or go to the bar, or have a cold beverage served out by the swimming pool, which was a big deal on a hot summer day, especially on weekends.

The bar was large and nicely furnished. You could sit down at the bar or a table or cozy and intimate booths with a view of the pool. Lunch and dinner were served in the bar from 10:30 am till closing time at 11:00 pm. Naturally this became the place to gather. Many of the lawyers (of which Laurel had too many) and business types were always there at lunch time waiting for the doors to open. Some ate lunch, had a drink and left. Some just came to have a drink. Some, like Bubby, just became a regular all day customer.

Bubby's regular group of pals would sit at the same table every day, five or sometimes six days a week. This group of guys were always telling jokes or talking about current events or local news, and with phone booths just outside the door, these guys could carry on their business and no one would know they were not in their offices.

Laurel has always had an oversupply of Lawyers, resulting in a good many hanging out at the bar waiting and wishing for something to do. One such attorney was from Texas and had married a lady from Laurel who was the only daughter of a very well to do family. This guy never had a client or a case, to my knowledge, and was the most boring, loud, rude, crude, pompous jackass I had ever met. He always had an opinion on everything and thought that he was a real live genius.

He was avoided by everyone, but would come in the bar at opening time and bother everyone in the bar. Moving to another table did not discourage him at all. He would just follow, and keep talking and bragging about his wide range of knowledge on everything and everybody under the sun.

One spring day I was sitting with Bubby and his group when this guy came in the bar. Bubby was badly hung over and not feeling good at all. He looked up and saw this guy come in the door.

With a sigh Bubby moaned," Oh lord, if the Doctor told me I had only 30 days to live I would hunt this guy up and spend every second with him." We all stared at Bubby in shock. He said, "CAUSE IT WOULD SEEM LIKE ETERNITY"!

THE GREAT DEER HUNT

For many years I have made a practice of reading the Jackson
Mississippi Clarion Ledger newspaper even though I hate
their editorials, and the leftist slant they spin on all the news,
but it is the major source of news about our state of
Mississippi. And I am always interested in what's happening
in my state, good or bad.

I always glance at the obits, not just to make sure I am not
listed, but also to see if any of my friends have passed away.
Having lived in this state for about 60 years and having a very
large extended family, many times I will see a name that I
recognize or have known in years gone by, sometimes I see a
name that brings a smile and good memories, not a smile at
the passing, but memories of a happy time, or good fellowship
or just having known a good person. Though sometimes a
little smile tugs at my mouth over the passing of some one
that I did not like, or who I thought had done me an injustice
in times past.

Recently in perusing the Obits I saw the name of an old
acquaintance that I had not seen or thought about in about 40
years and he is the subject of this little story.

The Mississippi Department of Wildlife and Fisheries have
done a splendid job in managing the deer population in

Mississippi. Nowadays anyone who goes deer hunting will see plenty of deer and most likely kill a deer if he or she can hold a gun or bow. I see in the papers all the time where 8, 9, and 10 year olds kill deer. All up and down the highways you can see the bodies of deer that have been killed by cars and trucks in many areas of Mississippi. The deer population has grown to such an extent as to be real pests, eating people's gardens and losing the fear of human contact. This state of affairs was not the case 40 and 50 years ago!

I spent most of my youth outdoors. We played outside in the woods all day when the weather permitted; certainly all spring, summer and fall .We camped out (spent the night) in the Tallahala swamps, the Leaf River bottoms, and the Boguehoma lake and creek banks. Sleeping on sand bars and swimming and exploring all day, I can only remember seeing 2 or 3 deer in all my teen years! A hunter who killed a deer was renowned all over the county. I knew plenty of men who hunted for many years and never killed even one deer! Some of my friends would hunt all deer season and never even see a deer! A hunter who had multiple kills stood in rare company, and was looked upon as a fine hunter.

One cold night in a Hattiesburg tavern, I sat with a group of guys who were planning a deer hunt. It was in the early 1960's and one of the guys was a real hunter. He was alleged to have killed five or six deer in his life. I personally did not believe this, though I would concede three deer because he went deer hunting all the time, it was his winter time hobby.

They were planning this hunt, south of Hattiesburg, at Brooklyn, Ms. on land that was in the Desoto National Forrest. When you hunted on "Guvment" land, as it was called back then, you had to enter by a checkpoint where the Game Warden checked your car and gun and when leaving you had to exit by the same check point and be searched again!!

As these plans we being made in walked a guy I knew from my high school years. He was quite a dandy in the mid 50's. In our High School years we all wore Levis and tee shirts. Chalmers wore nice dress pants, nice shirts, and had longer combed hair that was neatly trimmed. We all had flat tops and wore penny loafers with white socks while he wore dress shoes that laced up with dark socks. He was one of the guys, albeit somewhat different. As soon as he finished high school he went to work for a large loan company as a manager trainee and continued his habit of dress, adding a tie to the daily dress code.

Somewhat as a joke the famous deer hunter asked, "Chalmers, how 'bout you joining us on the deer hunt this weekend?"

After a moment's thought he replied, "I don't have a gun, or I would join y'all."

Quickly the deer hunter retorted, "I have an extra 12-gauge pump I will loan you." So, Chalmers agreed to meet the group at a Hattiesburg restaurant at 4 am Saturday morning.

This early hour would enable us to be at the checkpoint to be admitted to the "Guvment" hunting area just before dawn. Earlier in the year we had staked out spots where we thought deer might wander by. Each spot was called a "deer stand". To ensure that Chalmers would not accidentally shoot one of us we put him at the bottom of the hill near the entry road just out of shotgun range from the rest of us.

Just as the sun began to rise and I could see more than a few feet I heard a rustle in the underbrush. I raised my gun and then daintily tiptoed into my view one of the most beautiful sights in the wild; a small, petite doe with two tiny spotted fawns, little bitty things not even knee high, trembling in the early morning chill. They could not have been a month old, and the little doe paused, sniffed the air then carefully led the little fawns down the hill. As I sat there thinking what a sight to see, this must have been the doe's first offspring. She looked so young and fresh and alive, so attuned to her surroundings.

Suddenly my reverie was shattered by three blasts from a 12 gauge down the hill, BOOM, BOOM, BOOM!!! Horror of horrors, down the hill was where we had left Chalmers. Surely not! I thought, even a hunting rookie would not shoot a doe!

I rushed down the hill and was greeted by a sight that struck me dumb. There was the little doe and both fawns, all three dead, and Chalmers with a huge grin on his face. Before I could speak, he nearly shouted with glee, " I don't see why y'all make such a big deal of this deer hunting thing. It is not even 7am and I have killed three!!!"

It took an hour or so for us to figure out what to do. First we explained to Chalmers what he had done and the terrible consequences of killing a doe and fawns; Federal fines, confiscating his gun, jail time etc. name in the paper, losing hunting license etc., etc!

Chalmers was glum and defensive about the deal, "Hey, nobody told me," he said, "a deer is a deer. Why the big deal?"

Finally we buried all three bodies using our knives and sharp sticks, which took two more hours, then made good our escape, lying to the game wardens, saying we had missed when he remarked he had heard shots. Chalmers grumbled all the way home about his deer and not being able to keep them!

MY LIFE WITH GOUT

I have always been a healthy person. I am not subject to aches and pains, colds, flu, headaches, stomach disorders and other ailments. When folks would complain of this and that being wrong with them, I would shrug my shoulders and express a halfhearted, "Hope you feel better." Even as a child I escaped most afflictions of youth other than self-inflicted wounds such as falling out of trees, wrecking my bicycle, or jumping out of the loft of my grandfather's barn onto the back of his old mule, Jack. A real serious mistake, as Jack had never been ridden and did not like the idea at all. As a youth I healed up rapidly so in a day or so was back to doing things that all young guys do.

At age 15, I got my first driver's license and promptly wrecked the old Ford I was driving, destroying the Ford and nearly myself in the process. But other than accidents, wrecks, etc., I was never sick, did not feel bad or have anything wrong with my body. I played basketball, football, tennis, swam, and considered myself somewhat of an athlete. I played basketball with my kids up into my late 30's or early 40's and could hold my own. I took up racquetball about age 40 and really liked to play, played it three or four times a week. I swam and boated in the summers and thought I was the very picture of health.

One Sunday night at about age 45 I went to bed after an absolutely normal fall day. At peace with the world, I climbed into bed and began to sleep the sleep of the just. Somewhere around three in the morning I began to have this nightmare that someone was driving a nail through my right big toe. The pain was so severe that I woke up in agony. IT WAS NOT A NIGHTMARE! My right big toe hurt so bad that I sat straight up in bed and began to examine the offending toe. It was HOT to the touch and twice its normal size. The pain was so severe I could not believe anything could hurt so bad and still be attached to my body. What in the world was happening here? I got up and limped to the kitchen thinking I must have stumped my toe sometime during the day and forgotten about it.

With the pain not getting any better, I decided to soak the painful toe in some ice water, my old remedy for an injured member (sprained ankle, stumped toe, etc.). Sticking the swollen toe in a bucket of ice and water was a real error!! The pain went up at least 10 notches. I let out a howl of pain and dropped that idea. Gritting my teeth, I went back to bed and tried to sleep. (I have always been a sound sleeper.) WRONG ANSWER. No way to sleep. The pain was so bad I could not let the bed sheet or blanket touch the hateful toe. Tense and racked with pain, I resolved to hunt up a doctor to visit. I had moved to Hammond, Louisiana, several years before and did not even know a doctor in the state of Louisiana.

I called a friend and asked about a doctor. After several ribald comments about what ailed me, he referred me to a local MD. Arriving at the office, I was not first in line, and so had to wait for about an hour of pure agony while the doctor did whatever to the several little old ladies who were before me, all who seemed to be in no discomfort, while I sat there enduing the torments of Hell. Finally the doctor called for me. I painfully limped into his office in my bedroom slippers. In his best bedside manner he said, "Well, what seems to be the problem here?"

I gently eased off my sock and proffered my swollen, feverish member for inspection. "I have somehow injured my big toe, and I do not know how or when this happened!"

After staring at the toe for a moment, the doctor, said, "You, sir, have the gout. I can give you some pills to help the pain and lessen the duration of the attack, but there is no cure for the gout. You will have to change your diet, cut out red wine, no shellfish, no brandy, no rich foods or desserts, no red meat, no pork, no organ meats, etc." I sat in stunned silence for a minute.

"But how did I catch the gout? And when, and why so sudden?"

"The gout in some cases is inherited," the doctor explained. "Does anyone in your family have the gout?" I remembered my father complained some years ago about pain in his toes, and with the ignorance of youth, I just thought he was getting old and had arthritis or something.

"What do you mean change my diet? I eat crawfish, crab, oysters, gumbo, and redfish every day and have not had this before. Besides I drink very little wine and brandy. Scotch and gin and tonic are my drugs of choice with some beer to chase them with."

Then he added, "Oh yeah, and no scotch. Also, take these pills, one in the morning and one at night. Oh, and by the way, this medicine causes some people to have severe gastric distress after a while, so do not take them for a very long time or more than the daily dose."

Reeling with shock and sick with pain, I stumbled out of his office, hurting so badly that I gulped down two of the pills in hope of some quick relief. I had already taken six or eight aspirin and four or five Tylenol, plus two or three of whatever else was in the medicine cabinet. The very thought of giving up shellfish, booze, all things I loved to eat and ate every day was making me dizzy. What would I eat? What would I drink? I began to call everyone I knew in hope of finding some info about this dread malady. Everyone just laughed and said, "Gout is a rich man's disease; rich foods and drink are the cause!" I am not nor have I ever been rich, so I knew that part was not right. I resolved to find out all I could about the gout in hopes of averting another attack.

First thing I learned was that, yes, the medicine he gave me would, if taken too often or too long, cause such a stomach ache and diarrhea as to make it a tossup as to which was worse, the cure or the ailment. Second, I learned that while all doctors do not agree on the treatment of the gout, all agree that the formation of uric acid and the settlement of the uric acid crystals in the extremities is the cause of the gout. But what triggers the attacks and why? All I got was double-talk. Diet? Inherited? No one knew for sure.

The gout has been written about since the times before Christ. Roman and Greek scholars wrote long documents; even plays were written about gout as early as 200 BC, all through history. Gout has been discussed, cussed, even praised as a malady that only high quality, high intellect folks contracted. The very early writings about gout describe the onset and symptoms exactly as mine occurred.

After about a week of eating nothing but lettuce and tomatoes, beans and peas, and drinking water, my attack went away. After several more days, I went back to my old eating habits. A little at a time, I added the things I liked back to my diet. In the meantime I read any book I could beg, borrow, or steal about the gout. I asked everyone I could find who suffered from the gout to share any and all info about our common enemy.

I have had attacks through the years and find no common thread. I have tried every diet I have read about, heard about, seen on TV, or in health magazines. I ate enough cherries one year to fill the Super Dome after being assured by a friend that cherries were the sure cure. I still like cherries, but I had one of my very worst bouts while eating cherries by the boxcar load. I have changed diets from no fish, no shellfish, no meats, no pork, NOTHING GOOD, and have had attacks in the middle of these diets.

Thirty years have passed since my first attack, and now when I have an attack it is only in the winter!! All doctors say that is of no import: summer or winter makes no difference. Yet, it has been over a year since my last attack, February, 2013. It was very brief and mild compared to some, and before that I had an attack in January of 2012 which only lasted about 6 days! Nothing since February 2013, over one year ago! My diet does not change from summer to winter. I eat pork, shrimp, crabs, crawfish, gumbo, steaks, cheeseburgers, raw oysters, peas, beans, and cornbread, cracklings, ham, Spam, and highly seasoned stuff like chili.

I have come to the conclusion that gout does not know or care what you eat. If your uric acid chooses to act up and not do right you will have the gout. But what triggers the uric acid to go wild I do not think anyone knows. It strikes some people for the first time in their 40's, some in their 50's. Last month a friend, aged 62, called me and said he had heard me complain about the gout for so long that when he wakened in the night with a pain in his big toe, he knew what had happened. He went to the doctor and was told that the meds I had taken for so many years were no longer available and had been replaced by a med that cost $400 for a month's supply. Plus, Medicare does not pay for gout meds and most insurance does not pay for gout meds or treatment.

I recently went to visit a friend in the hospital who had gall bladder surgery. In the hospital for a week eating the bland soft diet they served, he came down with the gout. How can you explain that??

If you have the gout, you have my deepest sympathy. I do not know of anyone who has ever been cured, just some lessening of pain and longer between attacks. However, gout does make a somewhat better man of you; a man who has the gout prays a lot, and has sympathy for pain.

And why do so few women have the gout? No one answers that. There have been a few women, but very few who have been confirmed to have the gout.   Maybe God thinks that women suffer enough what with having to give birth to all mankind and having to put up with us men.

FOOD

I have always loved good food. As a child I watched my
mother (a true master chef) lovingly prepare and cook cheese
soufflé, pineapple upside-down cake, ambrosia, fresh yeast
rolls, turkey and delicious cornbread dressing with giblet
gravy, chicken and spaghetti, and sour cream pound cake, to
name just a few of our favorites. She made her own cottage
cheese and wonderful salads, all with flair. And of course, we
had all the usual: fried chicken, cornbread, fresh vegetables
and fresh fruit, all beautiful to see, smell, and taste.

I always felt very much at home in a kitchen, so at an early age
began cooking on my own. I fried, grilled, and roasted wild
game and fish. I began making gumbo, jambalaya, and red
beans and rice. Chili became one of my favorites, and I have
won several Chili Cook-Offs. (I am convinced that my chili is
the best in the world!)

In my early 40's I moved to South Louisiana and found that I
was a rank beginner in cooking; a mere novice, if you will. I
discovered stuffed artichoke, fresh Italian sausage, many
types of oyster stews, pasta, and red gravy, as opposed to
white or brown gravy; how to use fennel, oregano, basil,
rosemary, and fresh peppers. I learned to cook shrimp,
crawfish, oysters, redfish, soft-shell crabs (still one of my
favorites), all types of seafood, plus ducks, alligator, raccoon,

nutria, frogs, and other assorted creatures of the swamp. Under the guidance of my sister, who lives in St. Francisville, I learned the patience to make a roux. One good thing about roux, if you mess it up, throw it out and start over, as you have only wasted a little shortening and flour, and a bad roux will ruin anything you put in it.

Living in Destin, Florida I loved to eat everything from the Deep Blue. I ate oysters, shrimp, mullet, cobia, snapper, grouper, amberjack, triggerfish, stingray, and shark, fried, baked, broiled, grilled, smoked, and raw.

I learned to throw a net and caught lots of various types of fish. Once when fishing with a buddy I kept catching hardhead catfish, which everyone always threw back. Looking at them I wondered why everyone always threw them back; this is just a catfish. "Throw them back," my buddy said. "They are not good to eat!" Having caught very little that day, I decided I would keep them. I had caught a dozen or so, and when I got home, I promptly fried them, and guess what? Just a fried catfish! Smoked mullet is a real treat when you can find it. I would eat seafood every day if I could.

Living now in Senatobia, Mississippi, everyone cooks and eats all types of barbecue. A pork shoulder smoked on a grill for about 10 hours over hickory or cherry wood is a true delight. Several months ago a friend of mind and I decided to cook a goat. Checking around, we found a guy from Lebanon living near us who raised goats and sheep for the Mid-Eastern people in our area. We visited him and purchased a young goat, sight unseen. He was to kill, skin, gut, and quarter same, as part of the deal. Paying in advance, we agreed to be back the next day.

Arriving at the farm, we went in to claim our goat. A different guy was there. "Here is your sheep," he announced proudly. "Hold it!" we exclaimed. "We ordered a goat, not a sheep!" He looked confused, setting a large box on the counter. "But I have killed a young male sheep for you!" After much confusion, ranting, raving, cursing, shouting, and threats to world peace, we accepted the sheep. Not telling any of the 25 guests we had invited, we started preparing the goat/sheep. We soaked it overnight in our homemade marinade, then rubbed it with our pork shoulder dry rub and put it on the grill to smoke. 10 hours later, we served our sheep/goat to our guests. Everyone raved about how juicy and tender the "goat" was.

I do not want to eat, nor do I knowingly or willingly intend to eat anything that is Lite, low-cal, low-carb, low-fat, sugar-free, gluten-free, lactose-free, fat-free, organic, hydroponic, or healthy-certified. I am not rich enough to eat health foods, nor do I have any health problems (not counting gout), so I will just eat as I have been eating for the past 77 years, and hope for the best!

BAR-B-QUE

Growing up in South Mississippi (Vancleave, Mount Olive, Laurel, and Hattiesburg), BAR-B-QUE was an event (sometimes all day and night), or just a cook-out, or just a dish.

One of my very early memories was about 1943 or 1944, when we were living at Vancleave where my father was the Methodist minister. One fall afternoon my father came in and announced that the Church was sponsoring a Bar-B-Que. This event would take place between the Masonic Hall and the Turpentine plant, about a fourth of a mile behind the Church. I was very pleased when my Father said I could go with him to see to the preparations.

We walked the short distance (our parsonage was right beside the Church) to the open field where a group of men were very busy scurrying about. Several guys were digging what looked like a large grave, about 4 feet wide and 8 feet long, and 3 or 4 feet deep. Several other guys were chopping up hickory wood into pieces about 2 feet long and about the size of a piece of stove wood. This wood was piled into the pit as it was called, and set on fire; soon there was a raging fire.

They kept piling on the wood till the pit was about 2 feet deep with red hot hickory coals, then a lattice of iron work (looked like an old bedstead to me) was laid across the pit. Then from the back of a truck, wrapped in a bloody bed sheet, was a young calf, split down the middle from neck to tail, into two halves. These halves were laid on the metal framework over the coals, and a guy with a long-handled mop began painting on a sauce made from tomatoes, vinegar, mustard, brown sugar, pepper, salt and I do not know what else. One guy mopped and drizzled the sauce from a big pot perched over the coals at the very end. Then someone relieved him, as the coals were very hot. It was getting dark and my father said it was time to go.

"But what about the BAR-B-QUE?" I asked.

My father laughed and said, "They will be cooking and mopping all night long. We will eat tomorrow about noon."

The next day we gleefully walked down to the cooking site where some 50 or 70 people were gathered around the pit; the smell was wonderful. The calf was taken off one-half at a time and placed on a big wooden table, where a man with a sharp knife would carve you off a slice, placing it on a tin plate with a piece of bread, and drizzled some sauce on it. No utensils were furnished. Everybody had a knife, even we kids had a Barlow in our pocket. I can still remember the good smell and the tender beef with the sauce dripping down my chin. We wiped our hands on the bread and then ate it.

Later, as a teen living in the Laurel area, we frequently had a goat. BAR-B-QUE goats were plentiful and very cheap. A young nanny goat could be bought for $5.00 "on the hoof."

Then to get it killed, skinned, cleaned, gutted, headed and quartered was the next order of business. Most of the times the seller would do all this for you, for a slight fee. However, if you had obtained your goat through other than regular channels (It was an old joke in Jones County: "How do you have a Bar-B-Que? First you steal a goat.") you had to go into the neighborhood or to a poor person who would do all the above in exchange for the head, hide, innards, etc.

Goat liver was much prized in certain circles. Then we would marinate the goat overnight in a mixture of cheap red wine, hot peppers, tomato sauce, vinegar, and whatever spices we had lying around, starting the goat early in the morning over charcoal and hickory wood, letting it smoke and cook till late midafternoon. After lots of beer and lots of conversations we would partake. I am sure it was very good; at least I remember it being edible.

BAR-B-QUE is many things to many people. Living in the great state of Louisiana, I learned that as good as the food is (simply wonderful), meat cooked outdoors and slathered with catsup is not BAR-B-QUE, as many people in Louisiana think!!!

In the early 1960's, traveling all over the South, I was frequently in Memphis, Tennessee. One evening, after I had heard so many people bragging about the local BAR-B-QUE, I decided to try the favorite place everyone was bragging about. This was a place called LEONARD'S BAR-B-QUE. It had a drive- in area and you could place your order with the carhop. My server was an elderly black gentleman, very soft spoken and polite. "Order please?" he asked.

"I would like a BAR-B-QUE sandwich," I answered, "and by the way is this BAR-B-QUE beef or pork?"

He stopped, turned, and looked at me as if I had taken leave of my senses. "Suh!" he replied, "BAR-B-QUE IS PORK!!!"

Living now in North Mississippi I have come to love BAR-B-QUE. The Memphis in May World Championship BAR-B-QUE Cook-Off is a high spot in the year and I look forward to it each year. I have learned to BAR-B-QUE many things from goat, sheep (very good), chicken, deer, all parts of pork, but one thing still rings in my mind. "SUH! BAR-B-QUE IS PORK!"

THE SNAKE HUNTERS

Living in Hammond, LA and not having a powerboat was like not having any social life on weekends. Everyone went to the rivers and lakes Saturday and Sunday from about the first of May until the end of October. With Lakes Maurepas and Ponchartrain close at hand and big rivers every few miles emptying into the lakes, boating was a way of life.

The rivers were deep with wide channels and heavy cypress growth right up to the banks. The scenery is beautiful, the rivers slow and winding. The water was tea colored, yet clean and fresh right up to the point where it flowed into the lake. Lake Maurepas is separated from Lake Ponchartrain by a 5 mile channel flowing under Interstate 55 and Highway 51 at Manchac, Louisiana. Both Maurepas and Ponchartrain are fairly shallow for lakes this size, and both just teem with fish, crabs, shrimp, etc.

The rivers are scenic and empty of any sign of civilization except other boats and camps. On some rivers enterprising people have built bars with large docks that are accessible only by boats, and sell drinks, sandwiches, burgers etc. Some of these places have live bands on the weekends and draw huge crowds of festive boaters who spend the weekend riding from river to lake even crossing the lake to New Orleans, Louisiana, a 30 mile ride one way.

So, in the interest of recreating and after living in Hammond a couple of years, I purchased a used boat. It was alleged by the seller to be in excellent condition. It was a good-looking boat, about 18 feet long with a fresh painted, single axle trailer. It had plenty of room for 4 people and picnic supplies. The motor sounded good and cranked right up, which is not always the case with boats and motors. After testing this rig, my wife, Patricia, her brother Lanny, his wife Eleta and I set out to cruise the waterways and enjoy a pleasant Sunday. We put in at the Natalbany River at Springfield, Louisiana, a not so busy launch area. This would ensure my not being rushed and I would not be the object of scrutiny of so many experienced boatmen. This, I felt would enable me to get some experience at launching and getting out of the water. Also I would have the help of my wife's brother, who was an experienced outdoorsman. Also he owned a boat and could give advice to a novice such as I. After a real learning experience in backing a boat down a ramp, we got the boat in the water with no mishap, and headed down river.

This river was slightly smaller and had very little traffic, which was one of the reasons I chose this route. The river ran into the big river, the "Tickfaw" which ran into Lake Maurepas. it would take us about an hour to get to the big river so we just cruised along, taking our time admiring the beauty of the waterway. The river was so smooth and the majestic trees lining the banks, no other sign of civilization it reminded me of the scenes of an old Tarzan movie. After cruising a couple of hours, we decided to head back so we would have plenty of daylight to get the boat out of the water and get home before dark. Arriving at the boat launch area, I tied the boat to the bank and got the car and trailer and backed it down the ramp to the water. After several false starts, I got the boat positioned to go on the trailer. With the help of my brother-in-law, I finally got the boat on the trailer, got back in the car and started up the ramp.

Just as I got to the top and ready to turn onto the parking area, I felt a shudder and a sudden heavy drag on the car. I heard Lanny shouting "stop, stop". Quickly stopping and getting out, I discovered that my pretty trailer had broken in half, just in front of the axle. The nice white paint had only covered up the total rust through of the main beams on the trailer. The bottom of the boat was resting on the ground with complete separation of the trailer. We worried and sweated and jacked up the boat with the car jack to try to do something constructive. Several people tried to help but to no avail. Everyone advised us that without a professional welder nothing could be done.

We sat and lamented our fate. It was getting dark. It was Sunday. We knew no welders, and we were miles from any help or a phone. We sat listening to our wives complain about the heat, the mosquitoes, it getting dark, possible creepy crawlies, snakes, why did I buy a trailer that would break, and many, many more; but most of all no bathroom facilities.

Suddenly, an apparition came soundlessly walking out of the swamps, nearly scaring us out of our wits. Two men dressed in black rubber knee boots of the old farm type, blue jeans, plaid shirts, kerchiefs tied around their heads, revolvers strapped to their waist. But most amazing of all, both guys had 4 or 5 cottonmouth snakes hanging by their heads from their belts.

Both guys were Native Americans judging from their looks. They stared at us while we stared at them. "Y'all got a problem," the taller one announced.

"Yes", I said, "looks like we do and have no idea how to solve it."

"Well, first you need a welder" he said.

Lanny laughed and said "yeah, any idea where we could find one?"

"Well, as a matter of fact, my brother and I are welders, and our truck with all our equipment is parked just about a mile up the road."

"How much would you charge us to fix the Trailer?" I asked.

"How much beer do you have?" was his reply.

We quickly rummaged around and said "nearly a case!"

"Well, that will probably will be about right." He said.

I took them up the road to get their truck and asked about the snakes. "This is a hobby," they said. "We make belts and hat bands from the skins. We hunt snakes most Sundays in the swamps. Would you like to join us sometime?" I declined using some lame excuse. When they got back with the truck they jacked up the trailer and began to weld. They took turns. One would drink beer and talk to us while the other one would weld. Then, at some unknown signal, they would swap places.

It was very dark and I had the car lights on for the light and comfort. Patricia offered them a sandwich which they accepted, but stopped all welding activity to eat sandwiches and drink beer. Eleta kept asking where are the snakes they had and were they sure they were dead?

Suddenly, the taller one stopped welding and said, "it is as good as new, all done." We thanked them and offered to pay but they declined and said the beer and sandwiches were enough.

With us thanking them, they drove off. As we loaded up to leave, I said, "boy, I need a beer."

"No beer!" Lanny said. "The last one and the last weld went down together!" If there had been more beer we would still be at the landing.

I told this story several times in the Hammond area, but no one knew or had heard of two Indian welders that hunted snakes and drank beer. I was just grateful that they wandered up at our site!

MONA

In mid-1977 I moved to Hammond, Louisiana. It sticks in my mind because it was about 90 days before Elvis died. My move to Hammond was due to a reversal of my financial status and I was sure this move would guarantee my return to power. Hammond is a great place to live being 45 minutes from Baton Rouge and about the same to New Orleans.

Hammond is blessed with Southeastern Louisiana University, a school at that time of about 10,000 students, and Interstates 55 and 12 cross at Hammond which gives access to about anywhere in that part of the world.

I was working hard all day building a new business, so did not get around much at first. About the only place I would go after work was to the Holiday Inn bar. The bar was very nice and usually had a good crowd from about 5 till about 9 pm. The restaurant had good food and you could order in the bar. I was usually a late customer. After working all day, then getting cleaned up, I would arrive about 9 PM or even later.

I quickly learned that the two girls who worked the bar were students at Southeastern. They always had their books behind the bar and when the happy hour crowd thinned out would take turns studying. I would eat and watch TV as the girls studied and tended bar. As I was a regular and always left a tip, we became friends rather quickly. One night I commented on one of the girl's accent. I remarked that she sounded like a California Valley girl. With a laugh the girl, whose name was Mona, began to tell me her life story.

Mona was a true vegetarian and like all her type was thin and very pale. She was a gymnast and extremely agile, and graceful as a deer. She had bright blue eyes, long brown hair, and looked as if she were puzzled about everything. She talked slowly and deliberately, and was very polite to everyone, even the smartasses who frequent all bars. When someone annoyed her, she would look at them with the most puzzled look and say, "I don't understand. Would you please repeat that?" Most smartasses wilt under repetition.

She began her story with this statement. "I was walking down the street in South LA, California, going home after school my senior year of high school. We had been smoking some pot and a friend said, 'Here, try this.' I took the pill. My next conscious thought was, where am I? I awoke at the Baptist Hospital Drug Rehab Unit in Jackson, Mississippi and four years had elapsed. No joke, it was four years later and I had no idea how I got there or what had happened. Later I learned that I had lived in Colorado for three years and had been married at one time and divorced. I worked for a few months in Jackson, and made friends with a girl from New Orleans, so we came down here to work. I got my GED and enrolled in Southeastern. I work full time here and go to school. I am getting a degree in education with a minor in history. It is taking a bit longer because I have to work and go to school, and have no help. I never learned to drive a car so I ride a bike everywhere I go."

I was astonished by this story. As it frequently does in that part of the world, my next question was, "What do you do when it rains?"

"I just wear a raincoat," was the reply. "And rain water is good for the hair."

The other girl just laughed and said everything Mona had said was the gospel truth. They had roomed together and worked together for nearly four years. I began to add up the time frame and came to the conclusion that Mona was about 28 years old, although she looked about 16. When I asked her age, she said I was on the money, she was 28. But she said the years she spent "out of it" did not count, so that was why she looked so young.

I thought this was a great story and continued to be a regular customer at the bar. About a year or so later I wandered into the place one night and took my usual seat at the end of the bar. I was usually greeted with a cheery "Hello, McBride, want a beer?" But this night I noticed something wrong. Mona's eyes were red and she had a somber look. She acted like she was in a daze. I had to ask twice for a drink to get her attention. "What in the world is wrong?" I asked. Suddenly she began to cry silently, huge tears running down her face, dripping off her chin. "It's the end of the world, McBride," she sobbed. "It's my last semester of school and they say I must have about $400 at the Registrar's Office this week, or I won't be able to finish my last semester, and won't graduate. I just paid my rent and I have no money. What will I do?"

"Have you tried a loan," I asked, "or contacted your family in California?"

"No way, my family is worse than useless and no one will give me a loan."

I sat and drank my beer and thought of this girl in an unfamiliar place, among strangers, going to school for five years, trying to get a degree, and being this close: then the disappointment. After thinking about it a few minutes I called her over and gave her a loan of $400. Tears, elation, promises of never-dying friendship, pledging to repay as soon as was humanly possible and drinks on the house flowed for the rest of the night.

The next day I wondered if I would ever see my $400 again. But having faith in human nature, I just felt like everything would be OK. I would see Mona in the bar and would ask about school. "Things are going great," she would say. As I became more at home in Hammond, I found other friends and other places to go and went to the Holiday Inn bar less and less.

One spring evening I went into the bar, and to my surprise, they had a whole new crew. I asked about Mona and the other girl, and was told they no longer worked there. No one knew of their whereabouts. I inquired at the University and was told that, yes, Mona had graduated and had moved away. I began to berate myself. I should have known better; what a sucker I am. I will never see this person again. She just scammed me good. And so I just blew it off and went on with my life and work.

About three years later I was working at the Chevrolet dealership and had all but forgotten about the deal with Mona, when the secretary came by and said, "You have some mail." It was addressed to me in care of the dealership. I did not recognize the name on the return address. When I opened the envelope, to my surprise, there was a money order for $400 and a note which read:

Dear McBride,

I cannot get you off my @#*%*@ conscience. Here is your money. I am married and working in New Orleans, but I could not forget your kindness. Best of luck to you and many, many thanks.

Mona

With my faith in human nature restored, I went out to do battle with the world.

MR. BIG STUFF

In the late sixty's and seventy's, I was working for a large electric supply firm. This company had branches all over the Deep South, and as manager of the Laurel, Mississippi branch, I would frequently have to go to sales meetings at other locations. In mid-1971 we had a meeting in Baton Rouge, Louisiana. It was a weekend affair and was looked forward to by everyone in the company.

The Baton Rouge office was managed by a good friend of mine who always made any trip to Baton Rouge a memorable visit. His name was James, and he was originally from Meridian, Mississippi. He was small and wiry, rode motorcycles with utter abandon, drove his Porche like a maniac, drank and smoked anything he could get his hands on, would stay out all night, and then be at work on time the next day. Naturally, we became good friends. James had tattoos on both legs of a black panther climbing his shins; the blood running down from the panther's claws was most realistic. James talked very slowly and very quietly. You had to really listen to hear him.

His operation in Baton Rouge was the largest and most profitable of the company, and therefore, James could do no wrong. During the three-day meeting, James and I attended very few official functions, only the ones that the owner of the

143

company was sure to be at. Most of the time we spent exploring the bars and places that James knew so well.

The final day of meetings we were not at our best, due to late night carousing, when we were called from a meeting by the owner of the company. He informed us that an old friend of mine from Laurel was now the purchasing agent of a large corporation in New Iberia, Louisiana, and this old friend had requested that I pay the company a visit and set up a deal to sell them a large quantity of supplies. Since I had been requested by name and New Iberia was in James's territory, it was decided that James and I would jointly work the deal and we would travel to New Iberia the following week to set up the program. This was a great chance for us as we would be able to spend a week together at company expense. We would sell the supplies and party all night in New Iberia and Lafayette, which was virgin territory for me.

So the following week after several phones calls back and forth and coordinating with the purchasing agent of the company, I drove to Baton Rouge, and James and I set out for New Iberia in his company car.

As I had never been in this part of the world, I was very excited about this. We arrived in New Iberia about dark. It was summertime and very hot and muggy. After checking in at the motel and showering, we set out for a good time. The first bar we came to was separated from the highway by about a hundred yards of oyster shell parking lot. I remember thinking to myself, "What a huge parking lot for a place no bigger than this," but when we entered the place, it seemed to go on forever. The front was an old house, and the rest seemed to have been added on in a series of afterthoughts, certainly no rhyme or reason or planning had been used. The floor changed levels with no reason or warning, and rooms were attached for pool tables or other games, with no particular system or order. The front room, which was the main bar, was a sea of red Haliburton coveralls and silver hardhats, contrasting with the dark blue coveralls of the Schlumberger group.

It being the middle of 1971, James and I were dressed in the height of what passed for fashion in that disco-plagued time. We both had on loud polyester double-knit wide-lapel jackets, with brightly colored shirts, bell-bottomed double-knit hip-hugging slacks, with wide white belts and high heel patent leather high-top boots; mine were red - his were green.

As we walked into the big room, all conversation seemed to stop. Everyone stared at us as if we were from Mars. The juke box was blaring a song that was a great hit for Jean Knight of Jackson, Mississippi, and was Malco Records (also from Jackson) first hit. The song was "Mr. Big Stuff" and the refrain was "Who do you think you are, Mr. Big Stuff?" It seemed apropos and we in our disco splendor were the center of attention as we walked on up to the bar.

The coveralled hardhats just parted like the Red Sea and made room for us at the bar. The lady behind the bar was a buxom blonde with a great smile. She looked us up and down and said with a lilting Cajun drawl, "You ain't from around here, huh?"

With no little unease I said, "No Ma'am, but could we have a beer?"

"Honey, you can have anything you want from me, pretty as you are!" was her quick reply.

All the hardhats laughed and poked fun at her. One guy to my left said in a heavy Cajun accent, "I been coming here two years and she never even gave me a smile. You guys walk in like 'Mr. Big Stuff' and she falls all over you!"

With a toss of her blonde hair, she retorted, "You should try cleaning up sometime."

With a roar of laughter, the ice was broken. Suddenly we were one of the gang. Everyone wanted to buy us a beer and talk. I don't think the juke box played anything else all night but "Mr. Big Stuff." That song and Jean Knight are both imprinted on my brain.

In a few minutes our ties were off and we were shooting pool and dancing and singing with the best of them. I don't remember buying a drink all night. Every time my drink was close to empty, another one would appear as if by magic. James was having a great time showing his tattoos to the girls in the place and dancing with every female, regardless of age or appearance. I became more and more enamored of the buxom blonde who worked behind the bar. She had a wonderful sense of humor, was very bright, and handled the crowd with great finesse.

She and I became buddies very quickly. We would talk in between her serving, but we kept eye contact all the time, and her great smile just lit up the place. As the crowd began to thin out about midnight, we were able to talk more, and I don't think I paid for anything all night long.

Things began to get fuzzy about 1:30 AM or so, and the crowd was down to about twenty hard-core party types. The blonde suggested that we go to a place she knew that stayed open all night. After she closed at 2:00 AM or thereabouts, we loaded up in James's company car and headed out. At the new place we were greeted like long lost family because we were with the blonde, who it seemed knew everyone in that part of the world. She introduced us as "Mr. Big Stuff" and friend. Sure enough, the juke box was playing the same song.

We began shooting tequila and bragging about who could hold the most. My last thought was, "Boy, will I feel bad tomorrow!"

Suddenly I opened my eyes, with my head pounding in pure agony. My God, how I hurt! I was staring at the ceiling, lying flat on my back in a bed. Nothing looked familiar. The ceiling was all wrong. The walls had paintings that I was not familiar with. At first I thought I was in our motel then I noticed a painting of Jesus on the cross on one wall. Then to my horror, I saw a baby bed across the room and I realized I was in a strange room at a strange place, unclothed at that! Thank God I was in the bed alone, was my only thought. As I began to get dressed, every movement causing horrible pains to shoot through by head, I very gently opened the door a crack. Then I heard a "Psst!" and "McBride, McBride, where in the @#$%$#@ are we?!"

"I have no clue," was all I could mumble, when down the hall I could faintly hear voices and began to smell food cooking. What should have been delicious smells only caused my stomach to protest and heave. With great effort I swallowed and said, "Let's get out of here."

James agreed, and we began to try to find an exit. The house was very large and very nicely furnished. As we slunk around trying to find the outside door, we could hear talking and laughter. The smell of food and sometimes the sound of a small child crying made us very jumpy. Suddenly we opened a door to the driveway. There was James's company car.

As we started to the car, I noticed a broken baby bottle on the concrete driveway, then a bar glass, broken in bits, then several pieces of female clothing scattered in a trail towards the door, then obvious signs of someone being very sick. All this served to hasten our steps. Quickly we got the car started, and as we drove off, I looked the house over. It was a very large ranch style L-shaped house with nice grounds and large circle driveway. There was no name or number that I could see anywhere.

After a few mis-turns, we turned onto a highway that James recognized and made good our escape. I looked at James and said, "I am not sure how we got there. What do you remember?"

James said, "I remember nothing past getting into the car to leave the second place, and Jean Knight was singing 'Mr. Big Stuff' on the car radio. I remember we all sang along, and that is all I remember."

The rest of the week we avoided the bar from the first night and curtailed our night life. It took several days to get over the hangovers we had, and for some months after I could not listen to "Mr. Big Stuff" without getting a headache.

INANIMATE OBJECTS

For my whole life my most favorite personal sport has been punishing, cussing, torturing, and yelling at inanimate objects. I remember as a 8 or 9 year old kid working on my bicycle and getting so mad at the coaster brake when it would not line up to be bolted in after repairs that I took a hammer and beat the spokes out of the wheel, all the while yelling at and kicking the poor defenseless Western Flyer, till I grew tired and hurt my foot. My father had to take the bike to a repair shop and I was walking for about a week while all my buddies were riding, not to mention the whipping and talking to my father gave me, and at that age I had much rather have had the whipping than the long talk my father gave me about my temper tantrums.

I never considered attacking or cussing an inanimate object as a temper tantrum, only just retribution for the sins committed by the object. A case in point, when living in the great city of Hammond Louisiana one fine spring morning I was getting my boat ready for a season of fun and frolic on the lakes and rivers of the area. In my attempt to lube the throttle cable I was taking the cable loose from the outboard motor. The cable fit in a sleeve held in by a little steel pin, a simple twist and pull should free the cable.

Wrong answer!!

The cable would not release. I twisted and I tugged, I sprayed it with WD40, I put grease on it, all to no avail. By now I was hot and mad. After a few more frantic jerks I put a pair of vise grip pliers on the cable and used a tire tool in an attempt to prize the cable loose. With a snap, the cable broke at the housing and the vise grip pliers hit me right between the eyes knocking me backwards over the seat and onto the floor of the boat, flat on my back. When I struggled to my feet I felt a knot on my head like a hens egg between my eyes.

I quickly grabbed the offending Vise Grips and yelled at them, "WHAT YOU TRYING TO DO?? KILL A FELLOW?? I WILL FIX YOU GOOD!!! YOU COULD HAVE PUT MY EYE OUT!! YOU &%$%&## BLANK BLANK!"

I jumped down from the boat with the killer pliers in hand and grabbed a big ball peen hammer. Laying the murderous pliers on the concrete driveway I began to beat them with the big hammer, sparks began to fly and chunks of concrete and dust rose up. As I was screaming bloody murder my wife came out of the house telling me to hush, as the neighbors could hear me and would think I was crazy. I began to tell her the story.

She started laughing and said I WAS crazy, but be quiet so the neighbors would not know. I quickly retorted that I was a perfectly normal, well adjusted, middle aged man who had just survived an attempted murder and was wounded in the attack, and certainly was entitled to express himself, not to mention needing first aid and some sympathy, none of which was forthcoming, so I got some ice and nursed myself back to health.

Several years later I was living in Destin Florida (a true paradise on earth). One Friday night I begin to detect a slight tooth ache on the upper right jaw. As I was very busy repairing my crab traps, to set them for the weekend, I just ignored the slight discomfort and drank another beer to stave off any possible pain. About dark I went into the house and took two aspirins (My standard remedy for all things medical, up to open heart surgery) then sat down to watch the news on TV. Suddenly my toothache became a real serious matter!

I knew we had no toothache medicine in house so I headed out to find something to help. After visiting every grocery store, drugstore, 7-11, and bait shop in the Florida Panhandle I bought up all the over the counter tooth ache remedy I found. This was a once in a lifetime toothache, the kind you get when no dentist is available.

By now I was wild with pain, gritting my teeth and wanting to cry. After a sleepless night I started calling all dentists in the area, none worked on Saturday or Sunday. I even called the Local Hospitals trying to find someone who could or would help. Not one person offered to do anything except make an appointment for Monday morning. I spent Sat. and Sun. with tears in my eyes and my jaw throbbing from the top of my head to my shoulder.

That weekend I set a new world record for human consumption of aspirin, Anacin, & oil of cloves, not to mention beer, wine etc. I finally got to a dentist on Monday morning still in much pain, still tearful, but blinded with hate for the offending tooth. The dentist, a nice young man, oohed and aahed and finally said, "This is an upper jaw tooth, I think I can save it."

"NO!" I yelled, "I want it out, and I want it out NOW! I want that Sucker out NOW, THIS SECOND."

"You really cannot afford to lose an upper jaw tooth," Dr. Goldfarb said in his best Dental School bedside manner.

"I don't care if I have to eat Cream of Wheat or oat meal, or grits for the rest of my life! Get that blank, blank #$%*# out of my mouth NOW." He pulled the tooth, the second it hit the tray I grabbed it and put it in my pocket

After paying him what seemed a very small amount to me, for the relief of 2 1/2 days of horrible pain, I walked out into the sunshine and took a few calm steps down the street. But I could not wait any longer. I took the offending tooth out of my pocket and placed it on the sidewalk. I leaned over to speak to the tooth, "Had some fun did we? Well your fun is over you blank, blank no good blank, blank, #@%&#& you."

With that I stomped on the tooth with my right heel, and again for good measure. Looking down I saw that I had done no harm to the evil tooth, so scrounging around the gutter I spied a piece of concrete about the size of a baseball, "Ah! Ha!" I exclaimed with glee, "Gotcha Now Pal." Picking up the rock I begin to pound the tooth into dust, in the process getting my little finger smashed between the rock and the sidewalk, which brought a loud string of obscene words from my still numbed mouth. Flinging the rock away, I looked down at the tooth now just a pile of bone dust. "Now hurt somebody you lousy no good so and so!!"

I squared my well-adjusted, self-satisfied shoulders and cheerfully strolled away.

THE BAG LADY

Due to the drop in crude oil prices in the mid-1980's, the economy of Texas and Louisiana collapsed overnight, or so it seemed to those of us in the auto sales business. No one had a job or any money. Suddenly we all were looking at banks going broke, car dealers going broke, and industries closing. No one was buying cars. No one had any money. Jobs were scarce. The state of Louisiana laid off 2500 state employees in the Baton Rouge area in one month. The oil industry began laying off people every day. PHI (Petroleum Helicopters, Inc.) in Lafayette laid off 3,000 employees (pilots, mechanics, office workers, sales representatives) the same month. Suddenly we were all staring at bankruptcy and total ruin.

The guy I worked for at the dealership in Baton Rouge had always had a nice big boat, and we would fish the waters of South Louisiana, and sometimes we would go out front on an all-day trip, spend the night on the boat, and come back the next day. About a year before this total collapse my boss moved his boat to the Destin, Florida harbor and bought a house in Destin. He would spend the week in Baton Rouge, leave Friday noon for Destin, and come back Monday or Tuesday, leaving me to run things in his absence with things going from bad to worse. A new plan was hatched. We would all relocate to Florida. He would find a location, get things up and running, then we would shut down the operation in Baton Rouge and move to Florida. After a few false starts, we found a location in Fort Walton Beach, just across the street from the beautiful waters of the sound and fronting Highway 98, the main drag through Ft. Walton Beach, and across the bridge to Destin.

One cool, drizzly fall evening at our new location, I got a buzz on my phone to come to the owner's office. "What's up?" I said.

"Look out front. See that old bag lady under our new awning?"

I looked, and sure enough there was an old ragged, tattered female person with a grocery cart with what looked like all her worldly possessions piled on it and covered with some plastic to protect them from the rain and a piece of clear plastic around her shoulders and head. "I want you to go run her a** off. She is ruining the looks of our new front. She's dirty, and the salesmen tell me she stinks. They are all afraid to tell her to leave. She already cussed one of them out, and I need you to tell her to get the he** away from here and don't come back!!"

So out I go, walking slowly as the salesmen pointed, snickered, and giggled at it falling my duty to handle this distasteful situation. "Good evening," I said in my smoothest car salesman voice. "How may I help you, Madam?"

"You can make the %&*@ing rain stop so I can get to my daughter's house!" was the instant reply. I could feel all the eyes from inside the building on me and the old lady.

Just to stall for time and give me a breather, I asked, "Where does your daughter live?" I was thinking I might give her a ride as we would be closing very soon.

"Just out from Laurel Hill," she replied.

My heart sank, as Laurel Hill was about 40 miles north, past Eglin Air Force Base. "Well, there goes that quick fix," I thought. Still stalling, I said, "What you need is a car to get you there."

"Why do you think I am here, you d**** fool? I want to buy a cheap car, but none of your *&%@ salesmen would give me the time of day. They all run like I have a bad disease and will not talk to me, so &%^$ them!!"

Suddenly my brain shifted into gear. "Well, how much money do you want to spend for a car?" I asked.

"Well, I only have a little less than $5,000 in my purse, and I need to keep a little of that for gas, tag, etc, so what can you sell me for that amount? And I need something that has room for my stuff!"

Several days before we had taken in trade an old Volkswagen camper van. This was a real "hippie" van dating from the late '60's. The old thing ran good but was a true eyesore, painted a garish green and yellow with curtains on the windows, a sink, table, and two chairs, a two-burner butane stove, and a bed in the rear that let down from the top, plus a couch that made into a bed. We had very little invested in the old thing, and because it was so ugly it was parked around back out of sight. "You wait right here; I will bring just what you need, I promise."

When I drove back around I could see that she was excited. Opening the side door, I showed her how she could live in the van and have room for all her stuff. Even the shopping cart would fit inside. "How much?" she asked.

"I will let you have it for $4,500 cash today, with a full tank of gas." (which it already had)

"Done!" she replied.

When we walked back inside the building, the first thing I heard was "McBride, come to my office," on the intercom. When I got to the office, I could tell the boss was angry. "What are you trying to do, make this the Welfare Office? I want you to get rid of her, now!"

"I'm selling her the hippie van for $4,500 cash," I retorted, "and I want the full commission as none of the sales force would do anything to assist."

After a second of stunned silence he said, "Way to go, dude! Be sure and thank this nice lady for doing business with us. Do you need me to do anything?"

"No thanks," I said. "I can handle the rest of this deal."

After taking her money and doing all the paperwork for the van I walked her outside, leaving the door open to allow some of the bad odor to go away. I opened the door of the van, put the keys in the ignition and said, "Be sure to put the clutch in or have the van in neutral before cranking it."

I saw a strange look in her eyes, a look that made my heart sink. "I have never driven a car with a clutch," she said very slowly. "I do not know how to drive a stick shift." Visions of my $1,000 commission flying away nearly floored me.

Taking a deep breath, I calmly replied, "No problem. I will just teach you."

As it was now dark and closing time everyone else had left. I pulled the old van up to the front door where there was plenty of light. Cranking the old thing, I sat her in the driver's seat, nearly gagging at the unwashed body smell. I stood over her, gritting my teeth, and went all through the shift pattern, showing her how to pull up and move the shifter to find reverse. Then we worked on using the clutch, jerking and lurching forward to the street, then a panic stop, killing the motor, then jerking and lurching in reverse to the end of the lot, missing the clutch about half the time, gears grinding, tires squalling, as we jumped forward, then backward. Across and then back across the big lot we went. After a few hair-raising near misses with light poles, buildings, parked cars, etc., the old sister began to get the hang of it.

After about 25 sweat-soaked, scary minutes, we turned down a side street. I begged her not to look at the clutch every time she shifted, or stare at the shifter when she went from first to second. "Try to keep your eyes on the road at all times," I exhorted. Safely making a complete block for the third time, I breathed a sigh of relief and got her to stop and let me out at the front of the dealership.

As she lurched out of sight I said a brief silent prayer, crossed my fingers, and headed home as her tail lights got smaller down Highway 98.

I never saw or heard from her again.

THE IRONSIDES

My friend, Billy Frank owned in the late 60's and early 70's a fisherman's dream: a 40 foot, steel-hulled, twin diesel powered boat. This rig had once been an offshore crew boat which meant that it had at one time belonged to an oil company and had been used to transport men and supplies from shore to the oil rigs out in the Gulf of Mexico, thus was extremely sturdy and sea worthy.

This rig had somehow caught fire and all the cabin and supply compartments had been burned. The engines and hull were still good, just slightly rusty and gutted by the fire. All the controls and storage compartments were ruined and had been removed, leaving only an empty hull with two engines. Somehow Billy Frank talked the bank into lending him the money to buy this empty hull and transport it by big truck to a vacant lot in Ellisville, Mississippi. There it sat in all its rusty glory. It quickly became known as the "Ironsides" and the vacant lot became the "Ellisville Boatworks."

Billy Frank was an electrical contractor and a jack-of-all-trades. We became friends somewhere about 1965 or so. He helped me to learn to fly and would go with me on our flying trips about South Mississippi. He was a pilot of many years and it gave me confidence to have him sitting beside me on trips when I was a rookie pilot, even though I nearly killed us one time on a flight out of a pasture near Petal, Mississippi. His calmness and experience saved the day, but that is another story.

Being a contractor, and having many friends in all facets of the business, Billy Frank soon had all sorts of people working on his boat, all helping out: some out of friendship, some hoping to be invited on a fishing trip, some selling a product or service, though the few trying to sell something were soon made aware that no money would be forthcoming, because all cash and credit had been used up in the process of getting the rig to Ellisville. After 18 months of scraping and scrounging and remodeling, the Ironsides was trucked to the Tiki Marina near Tucci's fish camp at Gautier, Mississippi (pronounced Goshay to outlanders).

The Tiki had a great lounge and restaurant, plus well lighted and secure slips, with easy access to the Pascagoula River, hence to the Gulf and all the barrier islands which front the shoreline: Round Island, Horn Island, Petit Bois, Dauphin Island to the East, Ship Island to the West, then due south to the Chandeleur chain, which lie south of Ship Island, and stretch all the way down to the east pass of the Mississippi River. Breton Island and Freemason Island were frequent destinations below the Chandeleur chain, even though this would entail an all day trip, a night on the water, then fishing and all day trip back.

The process of rebuilding the empty hull into a fishing and pleasure boat required some modifications to the original shape. When completed, the Ironsides had a wheel house at the rear with a big open fishing area; then downstairs was a galley with a booth and a table like in a restaurant, a butane stove with three burners and an oven: a small stainless steel icebox and a sink, a storage compartment, the head, (toilet with flushing commode), then a room with four bunks and a small storage area. All the way to the front was the Captain's Quarters, Billy Frank's sleeping area, which had a full size bed with a night stand and a door to ensure his privacy.

All this being made of plywood instead of the original steel made the Ironsides ride higher in the water and go much faster than it used to. It was a real pleasure to go out front in it; the Ironsides just ignored waves which would have made a 25 foot pleasure boat bob like a cork. You could walk all around the wheel house and fishing area and not have to hold on or fear falling overboard.

After a few days of running around the local area, rivers, and calm waters a little way out, to get the bugs out and make final adjustments, it was decided to go out front on a two day "Maiden Voyage" Saturday and Sunday, run out front Saturday, fish the rest of the day, spend the night out on the boat, fish Sunday morning, then be back by mid-afternoon for the hour and a half ride home to Laurel.

After fueling up with 200 gallons of diesel fuel, which we all chipped in and paid for, loading several cases of beer, six fifths of whiskey, two of vodka, two of gin, two of rum, four loaves of bread, baloney, spam, mayo, mustard, ketchup, cheese, onions, eggs, cooking oil, etc. We were ready.

I was pleased to be included on this trip, as we had predictions of great weather for the weekend, and the prospect of catching lots of fish, and with good companions, it would be a perfect weekend.

Billy Frank, Toby, Johnny, and James made up the rest of the crew. We headed out very early in the morning just at daybreak. Johnny, who looked like a fat Drew Carey, was late. We nearly left without him, but he came lurching up just as we were pulling out shouting, "Wait, wait, don't leave me!" Turned out he had been out all night drinking and partying and was still very drunk. He could barely stand up. He was so funny we just couldn't be mad at him.

Johnny wore glasses so thick they looked like the bottoms of coke bottles and they always slid down on his nose so far you wondered what held them on. He was very bright and animated to the point of being hyper, loved sports and would bet his last dime on a football game or a horse race; he knew the betting line on every sporting event in the nation, and loved to fish and hunt. He was the only child of a couple who had him very late in life. These nice people were bemused by having a child so late in life and lost control very early. By his teen years Johnny came and went as he pleased, wrote checks on his father's account, wrecked the family car at least six times, flunked out of college twice, held numerous jobs and when in between jobs would just move in with his parents and mooch off them, treating the home and car as if they were his own.

About ten o'clock, the hot sun and the smell of diesel fuel burning was sobering Johnny up. The gentle motion of the boat, which I find soothing, was making him sick to his stomach. He solved this state of affairs by quickly downing about three beers, chasing them with shots of rum. By noon time, he was his old self again. When we broke out the baloney, cheese, etc., for lunch, Johnny declined, saying "Just a couple more beers for me, please, and I will be okay." Just before dusk, we decided to put a couple of lines out to troll for whatever. Johnny took over one line stating that he would soon catch a big something or other. "To catch a big fish you need a big bait," was Johnny's motto, so he reeled in the line and proceeded to change the bait and the hook. He demanded the biggest hook and the biggest bait on board. Sure enough Billy Frank produced a hook of giant size, stainless steel and shining about three inches longer than most hooks.

"Just right," Johnny exclaimed with glee. He secured the hook to the line, then reached for his bait. The bait fish had been frozen and was slimy as fish are when thawing out. With a grunt and a huge jerk, Johnny tried to impale the bait. Suddenly he moaned and bent over grabbing his left hand. The giant hook was embedded in the ball of his left thumb, the big barb out of sight in the flesh. Johnny sat down on the deck and stared at his thumb . We all gathered around to offer help. Someone cut the line and I managed to unsnap the swivel from the steel leader so only the hook was attached. After getting the boat stopped, we began to try to figure out what to do. Any touching of the hook produced screams of pain and pulling it out was not possible due to the large barb on the hook. Billy Frank restarted the boat and said we must press on as we were halfway there and could not turn back. Nobody had anything but an aspirin for Johnny's pain, so we decided to ply him with booze to try to ease the pain. This was the right idea for Johnny as he quickly began to chug shots of hard liquor. After about five shots the pain was eased and he got some relief.

It was pitch dark when we got to where we would anchor for the night. With the engines off and the little generator humming we had power for lights and the radio. The sea was calm and still. Everything should have been ideal, but Johnny was moaning and groaning and complaining, wanting to go back so he could seek medical attention. We all agreed that we did not want to cut short our trip, but something had to be done!

After careful consideration and some drinking, we concluded that we had two ways to get the hook out. Number one, take a sharp knife and cut his thumb to the barb then remove the hook. The other way would be to use pliers on the hook, then push the barbed part out, then cut the barb off and pull the barbless stem back out. Johnny vetoed number one at once saying that he did not trust any of us to cut into his thumb,

and he certainly could not do it himself. The other method
then would have to be done, so Billy Frank produced his
pliers and said, "Who is to be Dr. Kildare?" Johnny nearly
fainted at the sight of the big tool.

"Oh my God, I cannot stand this," Johnny moaned. "I will
need some more pain killer," was his instant cry, so we got the
rum bottle, as we all agreed rum would make you insensible
and oblivious quicker than anything in our pantry. Several
hard hits at the rum bottle later, Johnny said he was ready.
Billy Frank handed me the pliers and held Johnny's hand
firmly. James and Toby held Johnny's shoulders and other
arm. I grabbed the pliers and began to push the hook through
Johnny's thumb, ignoring the howls of pain which began at
once. I was surprised at how hard it was to push a sharp hook
through human flesh, when the hook made a tent of skin just
as it came through. Johnny with a low moan passed out,
which made my job much easier, finally getting the barb
through the skin. I tried to cut the barb off with Billy Frank's
side cutters; however, the stainless steel hook was very tough,
and every time I tried to cut it, poor Johnny would jerk and
twist even though he was only half conscious. At last the
snips cut through and with one motion I slid the hook back
out. Since Johnny was still semi out of it, we decided to
disinfect the wound by pouring vodka in it, but when we
poured the vodka into the open wound, Johnny sat up and
screamed and began twisting and jerking. We all just turned
loose and stepped back. Johnny jumped to his feet and began
flailing with both arms like a man possessed. His wild

swinging hit James on the side of his head as he tried to get out of the way. James was a big strong guy, and I guess reflexes took over and James put a perfect left jab on Johnny's chin. Lights out, folks. Johnny hit the deck like a sack of sand. His glasses bounced and the left lens broke into about six pieces. We gathered up Johnny and his glasses, repaired the glasses as best we could, and put Johnny into a bunk down in the cabin.

Exhausted, we all sat and had a drink and discussed this turn of events. What a way to start a fishing trip. We could hear Johnny moaning and tossing, so every few minutes someone would check on him to make sure he was alright and still breathing. About midnight we all decided he was okay and we went to sleep, hoping for a better day tomorrow.

THE WILD BLUE YONDER

During the early 60's when I would drive by the Laurel Mississippi Airport trying to drive and watch the airplanes taking off and landing at the same time was so dangerous to myself my passengers and all traffic on the road that many times I would just pull over, stop and watch, till I just had to go on to where ever I was going.

Laurel Mississippi has a fine airport built by the U.S. Army Air Corps during WW-2, long crossing runways with wide taxi ways and lots of approach room, plenty of space, big roomy hangers and acres of concrete paved apron provided local flyers with the best of everything an airport could offer. This was a really big time airport in our town and most of us just took it for granted, as it had always been there, or so it seemed to us. Many people in Laurel had planes and Gliders, Laurel being the hub of oil field activity in the state several oil companies kept their corporate planes hangered here.

Southern Airways had two flights through Laurel every day, one south and one north. Southern Airways flew the old DC3 in the smaller markets in those years, these were beautiful planes to me and I loved to watch them take off and land.

Laurel had a local FBO, which means fixed base operator, who supplied gas, oil, repairs, rented hanger space, rented planes, and taught flying lessons, flew charters etc. This FBO was

called Hesler-Noble Air Service. Mr. Alton Hesler and Mr.
Curtis Noble were both charter pilots, flight instructers,
mechanics, sold gas and oil, and parts. Both were U.S. Army
veterans who taught flying during WW-2 and had years of
experience.

They looked after the hangers, opened and closed the airport
every day, and were always available to answer dumb
questions about anything and everything pertaining to
Airports or flying. Mr. Noble was small, thin and very quiet,
and spoke in a low monotone. Because he was nearly deaf, he
wore a hearing aid which did not seem to help very much, so
you had to listen very carefully to get the message. He was
very intense and deadly serious about flying, and seemed
very old to me, as I was not even 30 at the time.

Mr. Hesler was somewhat dapper with blonde hair, just a little
gray and a mustache and much more outgoing and cheerful.
He would joke and laugh about things and people. I never
saw Mr. Noble laugh and he would smile on rare occasions
only. Mr. Hesler was mostly famous for having two beautiful
blonde daughters, who were very popular and well thought
of. True magnolia blossoms, Southern belles all the way.

One fine spring day in 1966 I could stand it no longer, and
drove up to Hesler- Noble Air Service and announced that I
wanted to learn to fly. Mr. Hesler told me to give him $10.00
and he would take me for a test flight for 15 minutes or so to
see if I had any aptitude to fly at all; for they were very busy,
and did not want to try to teach someone who would kill

themselves or others or would never learn to fly. They called these people, hanger pilots, who just sat around and talked about flying.

I forked over the $10.00 and we walked outside to a bright yellow and black Cessna 172. Mr. Hesler showed me how to do a walk around, check the tires, fuel and oil level etc. He explained to me with a smile, "There are no Shell stations in the sky" so check, double check, then check again. Cause you cannot just stop and walk home from a problem!!

Mr. Hesler sat me in the left seat where the pilot sits, and we went through the procedure for starting and checking the instruments, then we taxied out to the end of the runway, did a full 360 to look for any traffic, and headed down the runway. Suddenly we were flying. With my hands and feet lightly on the controls, I could feel the pressures on the control surfaces. After a few maneuvers, with his gentle prompting and reassuring tone of voice, I was flying the plane.

What a great feeling!

I was absolutely in heaven. Nothing I had ever done could compare with the joy of flying. Everything was so beautiful, the sky so clear l could recognize landmarks and roads and bridges from 2500 feet up. The cars on the highway below seemed to be crawling along and looked like toys. The South Mississippi countryside is pretty flat and I could see Hattiesburg 30 miles to the south, I was hooked!! After a few more minutes Mr. Hesler talked me through a 180 degree turn and we headed in. As we began to lose air speed and altitude Mr. Hesler talked me through a smooth landing.

As we taxied to the hanger he said, "Well son, looks to me like you can fly. You will be a quick and steady student. Come back tomorrow and we will begin your lessons.

Under the calm tutoring of these two (you never knew who would take you up for a lesson when you arrived) I quickly soloed and had my student license. I would fly every day that I could, sometimes only 30 minutes, but mostly 1 hour or more per day. I flew all over South Mississippi into Alabama, to the Gulf Coast, to the Mississippi river just to look, then home. I could not get enough of flying.

One hot August day, with the temperature about 100 degrees, I was sitting in the shade at the airport thinking of where I could fly, and old buddy wandered up. This guy was a general contractor and did a lot of building in the area, and was also learning to fly. Hello McBride he said "Want to make a $100.00 bill?"

"Only if I don't have to kill someone" was my reply.

He began to tell me the story of his having bought an airplane in Petal Mississippi. The airplane was Piper, 4 passenger plane alleged to be in excellent condition, but was located in a cow pasture near Petal Mississippi where the old owner had a homemade grass runway. At one end was a group of tall pine trees. At the other end was a very high voltage power line with big poles and cross members.

My buddy had very little flying time and said he was afraid to fly the plane out of the pasture, so his solution was to hire me to fly it to the Laurel airport about 30 miles away. I jumped at the chance to make the $100.00 so off we go to between Runnelstown and Petal just off highway 42. Sure enough, in a large cow pasture under a tarp, tied down, was a red and white single engine Piper, all shiny and clean.

A grass landing strip had been leveled down the center of the pasture, which looked very short to my young eyes. After a brief debate with my buddy about the power lines at one end, or the pine trees at the other, as no wind was blowing I decided that the pine trees were the best option. As my friend watched I fired up the plane and turned toward the pine trees, running it up against the brakes. I quickly got off the brakes and pushed the throttle all the way in. The grass strip was much rougher than it looked. As I was bouncing down the strip the trees kept getting bigger and I did not seem to be gaining much speed.

I knew that on a hot day it took longer to get airborne but I was getting pretty worried. The bouncing was getting worse, the trees were getting closer, so I gently pulled back on the yoke and after a real vicious bounce was suddenly airborne, but I had very little altitude and not much speed, so I nosed down to gain some speed, then pulled up and cleared the tree tops by about 6 inches!

My hands were shaking and my heart was pounding.

Just ahead I could see the highway to Laurel so I kept about 1200 feet of altitude and flew right above the highway till I got to the airport. After an uneventful landing I was sitting in the shade by the hanger when my buddy drove up. After handing me the $100.00 bill and thanking me I asked why he did not get the previous owner to fly it to Laurel as it was only about a 20 minute flight.

After a slight pause he looked down and said , "well this plane has had a bad habit of quitting on take-off, or not getting up to speed and he said he would not fly it under any conditions, anywhere, anytime, as no one could determine when or why it would decide to quit, or just not get up enough speed to fly and it needed the attention of a real good mechanic to find out why it would do these weird and unacceptable things, and I sure would not try to fly it!!"

Needless to say, we were no longer friends, and I don't think I ever spoke to him again!

SHINE

Recently I saw a newspaper article about a whiskey still having been found near a North Mississippi town. The writers were much amazed that such a thing still could exist in the modern world. I was also surprised as I had not thought of homemade whiskey being made for many years.

Growing up in South Mississippi, everyone knew someone who made whiskey. Jones County was for many years a real center of the whiskey making and distributing business. Every so often, usually during an election year, you would see in the paper where the local sheriff had caught some guy making whiskey. Big front page news, picture of the still on the courthouse lawn with all the law men standing around looking pleased; then, no more news for a couple more years. My father always said the picture was of the same old still; they just dragged the still out every time an election rolled around.

Jones County had a honky-tonk or juke joint, as many called them then, on every road outside of town. None were in the city limits. Inside the city limits, shine was sold mostly by blacks, and from small cafes or restaurants. The Country Club and VFW had open bars and controlled sales of whiskey in town. They sold bonded whiskey, not homemade, real stuff, like Early Times and Four Roses - even delivered. The farther

175

out in the county the joint was, the more likely it was that shine was the only alcohol sold there. Shine, as we all called it (never moonshine) was sold in 1/2 pint bottles for 50 cents each. That's right, 50 cents. A pint bottle was usually $1.25 (go figure): a fifth was $2.50, and a gallon was $10.00. All bottles were saved and reused. Kids could pick up used whiskey bottles, all sizes, and the joints would give a few cents for them. Many people scrounged the dumps and ditches to get the bottles for spending money. Gallon jugs were saved and stored in barns, rinsed, (allegedly) and reused.

A half pint of whiskey does not sound like much, but I can assure you, a half pint of shine and one Barq's Root Beer will absolutely mess up four teenage boys, and cause such chaos as is hard to believe. I think most shine was about 150 proof. I can still remember the burning as a swallow went down and the horrible after taste that lingered, 'til a big swig of Barq's Root Beer cut the acid taste. But nothing could modify the bad breath of a person drinking shine. Only time and chewing green pine needles would help!

Making homemade whiskey is not difficult, but one thing you need is a lot of sugar and some country stores made a lot of money selling sugar in 100 pound sacks. A dead giveaway was a guy driving up to a small country store and buying 500 pounds of sugar. The Feds began to monitor the sale of sugar at stores, so a big business arose in going to neighboring states and buying a big truck load of sugar.

When the corn, wheat, and oats were mixed with water and sugar to become the mash from which the shine was made, a smell arose that was very pungent. This smell lasted for several days as the mash worked and bubbled and seethed. To hasten the process, the still operator would sometimes throw a dead cat or other small animal into the vat. This would shorten the process by a day or so and cut down on your chances of being caught. As the mash was boiled and the steam caught and distilled into alcohol, nothing could get through that was bad.

Another problem was in the distilling. A copper worm (coiled tube) was used to catch the steam, causing it to condense into the liquid state and drip into the catch device. As copper was somewhat expensive and buying copper tubing in quantity was another giveaway, many shiners would take the radiator out of the truck and use it for the condenser. Big problem! Auto radiators had lead solder on all seams, and brass and copper and lead and other metallic salts were then exposed to steam and alcohol, forming a very toxic brew, that when ingested over a period of time caused a serious medical problem causing stroke-like symptoms, blindness, inability to walk straight, slurring of words, staggering, sometimes paralyzing the poor unsuspecting user. This condition was called "Jake Leg" or "Jake Leggedness." Some died from this condition. A real insult was to call someone a "Jake Leg," which implied that he only drank cheap homemade whiskey, or was affected adversely by drinking same, or was a "not so bright" person.

Several of my high school friends were the children of shiners or honky-tonk owners. I hung around these places every chance I got, much to my parents' dismay. I met some real strange people and learned some life lessons early on.

I remember one guy who NEVER IN HIS LIFE did anything but make and sell shine. This guy would get caught every now and then, but never stopped making shine. In the early 60's, when he was about 80 years old he told me that he had never had a driver's license, never had a social security number, never had a bank account, never registered for the draft, never filed a tax return, and had never owned anything in his name. But, he had a nice home, raised children, went to church, always using cash only. His wife had all deeds and titles in her maiden name. He lived into his late 80's, and left his children well off.

SOME THINGS I HAVE NOTICED IN THE LAST 78 YEARS

1-- I have never seen a cat skeleton in a tree

2-- I have never seen an armored car in a funeral procession

3--I have never been to a funeral of someone who died of a broken heart

4--I cannot trust a man who has no sense of humor

5--I do not trust a man who drives a Cadillac with slick tires

6--I do not trust a man who dyes his hair (coal black is the worst)

7--Some people hang around the Church all the time, thinking to hitch a ride? (standing in the garage does not make you a Car)

8--Profanity is a crutch, for a person with a limited vocabulary

9--Clean and neat is always in style

10-- If you exercise all day without altering your eating habits, you will only become a very strong fat person!

11-All ladies are females, but all females are NOT ladies! Also all gentlemen are males but all males are not gentlemen

12--Ladies, if you want to become a sweet little old lady, you need to start practicing about age 40

13--Young people today, have no social skills, or grammar, or table manners, or knowledge of geography, many have never seen a globe (72 percent of college students cannot find Spain on a globe)

14--Females will spend $100.00 on a new hairdo,$100.00 on a manicure, $100.00 on a new perfume, $350.00 for a pair of shoes, and handbag, $500.00 for a new designer dress, many thousands on diamonds and gold adornments, then scream Sexism if a man says, " My, you look nice"

15--When a man places his hand on his heart, rolls his eyes heavenward and says "TRUST ME", RUN!!

16-- A dog will usually not bite the hand that feeds it, This is the main difference between dogs and Mankind!

17--Family, faith, and Friends, become much more important as the years hurry by.

18--Intelligence and education are not the same, (I have met many people who were educated far beyond their mental capabilities)

19-- Growing old is not bad, considering the only alternative!

20-- Growing old is mandatory, growing up is optional!

21--Ignoring a problem does not make it go away!

A BRIEF OVERVIEW OF ISLAM

There seems to be a lot of confusion about Islam/Muslims in our world today.

The American Media, due to PC constraints, seems reluctant to (as we used to say) call a "spade a spade," as regards Islam. The media spends a lot of time trying to avoid connecting all the horrible crimes against humanity with these people, all of whom are Muslims! Even the President of the USA goes on taxpayer-paid TV and makes the absurd statement that "ISIS is not Islam" when the whole world knows that he is telling a bald-faced lie; "ISIS" is the core and essence of all that is Islam!

After the horrific events of 9-11-2001, I began to puzzle over what could motivate a group of people to kill over 3,000 folks they had never met or had any contact with: innocent men, women, and children, all strangers, only one common bond: all Americans.

I went straight to my local library, and checked out a copy of the Quran and began reading. (I now have 5 different translations of the Quran and have read them 25 times.) As I gradually got over my shock at the pure hatred on every page of this little book, I began to realize that Islam is so far removed from our thought process that we have trouble comprehending the deep and pervasive hatred of us that they are taught from birth.

There is no common ground between Christians and Muslims. The Quran states many times and in many places that God had no Son, and Jesus was a man. A good man, in fact a prophet, but a human, no more, no less. Muhammed was the last prophet, therefore his sayings, ARE the FINAL WORD! The benediction in all mosques worldwide is straight from the Quran, and is as follows: "Death to All Jews and infidels."

Guess who are infidels?

In fact Muhammed says early on in the Quran that Jesus was but an apostle of Allah, and there was not, and is not, a Trinity!

The Quran is a garbled collection of what are alleged to be the messages given to Muhammed by Allah. There is no order, time-frame, or sequence in this book. The longest chapters were put in first, then the shorter chapters; no rhyme or reason, just stuck in and numbered. If Muhammed said something in an early chapter, then for no reason changed it in a later chapter, the later (numbered) chapter rules!

Many quotes attributed to the Quran are from the other books that are considered holy: the "Hadiths, Ishaq, Tabari and Bukhari." These are sayings from Muhammed that someone is alleged to have overheard and repeated to a credible witness! Therefore Holy!

Muhammed could neither read nor write; all scholars agree on this. He was born 570 AD: died 632 AD. At his death he had

37 wives. His favorite wife was Aisha, whom he married when she was six (6) years old; however, gentleman that he was, he did not consummate the marriage till she was nine years old (9). He had many children, but none of his sons survived past infancy: all male children died soon after birth. Many scholars think they were killed so as not to be a threat to Muhammed's rule, in his life.

Muhammed knew many Jews and Christians and alludes to them frequently in the Quran. But since the Jews and Christians did not accept his teachings, they must convert to Islam or pay a lifelong tax and be second-class citizens, or Die! Any infidel is fair game for any Muslim to kill with impunity. No contract, treaty or agreement with an infidel is binding on any Muslim if he decides to abrogate it: said document simply becomes Null and Void.

All women are the property of some man as long as they live: their father till marriage, then their husband till death. All men are allowed 3 wives at any one time, and temporary wives, if not at home or no access to a wife. These women would be called prostitutes in other societies. A Muslim who dies in the service of Allah is entitled to 72 Virgins in Paradise, plus all the wine, milk and honey they want!

The Quran states that Allah gave the world to the followers of Islam; it is theirs and they can take it. Anyone who opposes Islam or renounces the faith can be put to death by any Muslim, anywhere, at any time!

It is not just Christians the Muslims oppose; it is ANYONE who interferes with the spread and implementation of a Muslim ruled and controlled world. There can be no civil law, no secular law, just Muslim Law, as shown in the holy books of Islam!

The Quran was written in such an archaic form of Arabic that it is unreadable today. Less than 1/2 of one percent of the Muslims today can read the Quran as written. Modern Arabic is today so differently written or spoken as to be a completely different language.

It would be like going to Rome and handing a young resident a letter written in Latin. He speaks and writes Italian, not Latin. Same with the Arabic of the Quran; imams in the mosque that teach, preach, and incite the Muslims to kill today spend twelve years committing the Quran to memory. So few scholars can read the Quran, as written, that they spend most of their time teaching imams, and conducting classes!

So much has been written and spouted on TV and social media about the Religion of Peace, and so much confusion about Islam, I will give a few illustrations of the types of Muslims and the positions they take in our world today:

1. The Peace-Loving Muslim. This is Hassan, down at the corner gas station/ convenience store, where you buy your gas, beer, soft drinks, cigarettes, and drive through the car wash. Hassan keeps a low profile,

smiles and takes your money and sends it to the mosque; they then send the money to wherever it is needed to buy explosives and train terrorists.

2. The Moderate Muslim. This is Akeem Mohammed Al Jabasr, the imam at the local Mosque. You see him in the paper from time to time, most often on the Sunday Religious Garbage section of the newspaper where liberal ministers all   make excuses for and apologize for the crimes of the Muslims, all calling Islam the religion of peace, most of whom have never read the Quran! Akeem is in charge of local propaganda, all PR, sending the money to the proper places, and finding young dummies to train and send to mid-east countries to learn to kill innocent women and children, and themselves, Praise be to Allah! Akeem stays home and makes talks on TV and to the left-wing university groups, organizes protests if anyone dares defame the Religion of Peace, drives his new 740 BMW, and sports his new young wife around!

3. The Radicalized Muslim. This is Al-Shaber-Mullah, born "Leroy Montgomery" in the hood, 22 years ago, a 5th generation welfare dude, been arrested 19 times. Things just ain't going to suit him, the man be after him, and everyone be against him so blowing up a

bunch of people and getting 72 virgins and a life of ease be right down his alley; been wanting to travel overseas and be a hero anyhow.

4. The Radical Muslim. This is Saleem El Shishkabob, 36 years old, born in Palestine, Iraq, Iran, Pakistan, Lebanon or wherever, taught from birth to hate all infidels. Has 9 children by 3 different wives, has no job, does not need or want one, has 3 AK 47's and 1500 rounds of ammo, gets food from the UN and US Foreign Aid, plus has 3 goats that give milk and live in the front room. Saleem is no different from any one of the billion or so Muslims in the world. He has been brain-washed in his mosque all his life and believes that there is no higher calling than to die in the Service of Allah, taking as many infidel's lives as he can!

5. The Everyday Ordinary Muslim. No different from any of the above. Everywhere in the world, Muslims are the same. Just as our army has truck drivers, cooks, lawn care people, office clerks, paymasters, laundry helpers, pilots, mechanics, every Muslim does not carry an AK 47 or have a bomb, but he is in the Muslim army, and is ready, when given a chance, to kill some infidels.

6. There are no Peace-Loving Muslims, no Moderate Muslims, no Indifferent Muslims, No Radical Muslims. Just Muslims. A Muslim is a Muslim. Period.

A DAY IN THE PARK

One fine spring day a guy is walking in the Zoo in Washington DC when he notices a little girl leaning into the Lions Cage. Suddenly, the lion grabs her by the collar of her leather jacket and tries to pull her into the cage, with mouth open wide, under the eyes of her screaming mother.

The guy runs to the cage and quickly hits the lion square on his nose with a powerful punch. Whimpering with pain the lion jumps back and lets go of the little girl. The guy scoops up the terrified child and hands her to her Mother, who begins thanking him profusely and endlessly. Several people watched this event. One was a reporter for a major Washington DC newspaper and writer for several publications.

The writer addressed the hero and said "Sir, that was the most gallant and the bravest Thing I have ever seen."

"Why it's just what any red blooded man would do. This child was in danger, and I did what I thought I had to do to save her. I acted as I felt I should and I hope any American seeing a child in danger would do the same."

The reporter said "I will make sure this does not go unnoticed. As a journalist I will see that this heroic act gets its proper due. Tell me about yourself?"

The guy replies, "I am a former US Marine. I am currently unemployed and looking for work. I am a staunch Republican and a regular church goer."

The journalist left to go to work. The next day the ex-Marine buys a newspaper and sure enough on the front page of the Washington Post the headline reads.

"Vagrant citizen assists with problem with small child in minor disturbance at Zoo"

He then Buys a Rolling stone Magazine and finds this article "Right Wing, Fanatic, U.S. Marine assaults African American immigrant and Steals His Lunch."

A SAVAGE JOURNEY THROUGH THE SOUTH

Much has been written about the swath of destruction cut through the South by Gen. William Tecumseh Sherman. Most historians and writers concentrate on the infamous burning of Atlanta and the subsequent "March to the Sea" ending with the surrender of Savannah and Sherman's gleeful telegraph message to Lincoln: "I beg to present you as a Christmas gift the city of Savannah, with 150 guns, plenty of ammunition, also 25,000 bales of cotton." Lincoln replied, "Many, many thanks for your Christmas gift, the capture of Savannah." December 1864.

As a long-time student of history, and having a life-long interest in the War Between the States, (I had nine ancestors who fought in that war – two for the North; both died in the service) I knew that Sherman was at the fall of Vicksburg on July 4, 1863, and began his quest to destroy and bring desolation to the South.

As I studied Sherman's life and role in the war, I began to see the deep and abiding hatred he held for the South. In his memoirs, letters, correspondence, and notes to and from his fellow officers, one message shines through. His desire was to punish the South and all her peoples in a way so severe as to make an everlasting impact. So many writers pass off

Sherman's destruction as just good military tactics, but all his personal writings tell a different story.

William Tecumseh Sherman was born in Ohio, the son of an Ohio Supreme Court Justice. At age nine, his father died and he was adopted by a family friend, Thomas Ewing, who became a US senator and appointed Sherman to West Point. (Sherman later married his adopted father's daughter, Ellen Ewing.) Sherman graduated from West Point, sixth in his class, in 1840. He served in several posts in the South and in California. Unhappy with the low Army pay, he resigned his commission in 1853 to run a bank in San Francisco. When the bank failed in the Panic of 1857, he went to work for a bank in New York; it too failed. Sherman then moved to Leavenworth, Kansas, and became a lawyer. In January of 1860, he took the post of superintendent of a new military school in Alexandria, Louisiana, called the Louisiana Seminary of Learning, later Louisiana Seminary of Learning and Military, later moved to Baton Rouge and became LSU.

Sherman fathered eight children and was noted as a devoted father. His oldest son, Willy, was always his favorite. His wife was Catholic and always wanted Sherman to convert. He spurned Catholicism, which strained the marriage. Sherman always said he was "cursed to live a vagabond life." Sherman was a gifted artist and mapmaker and sent many drawings of the places he went and things he saw. His rise in the ranks of the army began when serving with Gen. Grant in the two battles for control of the Mississippi River during the siege of Vicksburg.

When Vicksburg fell on July 4th, 1863, Sherman was elated with the victory and the part he played in it. He sent for his wife, Ellen, and the four oldest children. During the reunion, Willy caught typhoid fever and died. Sherman was devastated, and this solidified his resentment of the South into cold hate. Just after Willy's death he wrote, "Any who support the Confederacy deserve to be treated as criminals. To those who submit to our rightful authority, all gentleness and forbearance, but to petulant and persistent secessionists, why, death is mercy, and the quicker he or she is disposed of, the better."

For Sherman, the fight against the South was personal as well as professional. It did not just involve hostile armies, "but a hostile people," whose pride in home and cultures was to blame, as much as politics. He believed he possessed an understanding of southern manhood and, therefore, the stubbornness of the conflict. His years being the superintendent of the La. School gave him insight. He said, "I know well the young bloods of the South," as he called them. "They are the sons of planters, lawyers, men about town, good billiard players, sportsmen, who never did any real work and never will. War suits these men. They are brave rascals, fine riders, bold to rashness, and dangerous subjects in every sense. They care not a cent for Negroes, land or anything. They hate Yankees, per se, and don't bother their brains about the past, present, or future. As long as they have good horses, plenty of forage, and open country, they are happy and they are the most dangerous set of men that this war has turned loose on the world. They are splendid riders, first rate shots, and utterly reckless. These men must all be killed or imprisoned by us before we can hope for peace. Nothing short of total devastation would cure them of fighting." Sherman believed, "We must make them so sick of war that generations will pass away before war would again appeal to them."

Together with Grant, Sherman settled on a "strategy of exhaustion," calculated to demolish the homes and spirit that supported the Confederate war effort. "I will make this war as severe as possible. I will show no symptoms of tiring until everyone in the South begs for mercy." Leaving Vicksburg, Sherman's plan was to march across the width of Mississippi from Vicksburg, in a straight line, due east to Meridian. The plan was as simple as it was savage: "I will gut this state." He left Vicksburg February 3rd, 1864, with 20,000 men. In addition to weapons, each man had a pickax and shovel. He proposed to burn houses, barns, cotton gins, railroads, fences, crops in the fields, and anything the South could use, ride, or eat. Grant had already burned Jackson to such an extent that it was called Chimneyville. He ordered 7,000 more cavalry to drive south from Memphis to meet him in Meridian.

Sherman's men laid waste to everything they came across in this march from west to east, like a belt all across Mississippi.

Each day, parties were sent out to destroy dwellings, tracks, bridges, roads, barns, fields, and homes until the entire horizon was flat and smoking. Soldiers burst into homes, seized every article and morsel, even sweeping food off the table. These soldiers were intent on punishing all Southerners. A soldier named Lucius Barber of the 15th Illinois, observed, "The country was one lurid blaze of fire; burning cotton gins, dwellings, barns, and fields were seen on every hand, I regret to say, but oft-times habitations were burned down over the heads of the occupants. I saw the cabins of the poor entered and the last mouthful taken from the starving children as the cabin was burned." Sherman's men marched the 150 miles to Meridian in under two weeks.

The residents of Meridian hid behind locked doors and peered out windows as the Yankees occupied the town. A Meridian woman, Mrs. Ball, described the wrecking and ransacking that ensued in a letter to her mother that found its way into a newspaper, "The mob ran around breaking into houses, kicking down doors, tearing into trunks, closets, chests, tearing up and destroying everything they could. Caught all the chickens on the place in a few minutes." Five men broke into her house and demanded any arms, silver or gold that she had. They carried off all the blankets and bed coverings and food in the pantry. Every public building was burned to the ground, every warehouse, every store, all three hotels were burned. Not a cow, horse, mule, or chicken was left in the town or for 10 miles around. Not one fence or crib or barn was left intact. The Yankees then spread out into the

countryside 50 miles in each direction. Every unit was
assigned a portion to destroy. They pulled up the railroad
tracks and bent them around oak trees, rendering them
unsalvageable. They called them "Sherman bowties." For
five days, 10,000 men worked hard and with a will in that
work of destruction. Sherman wrote in his report, "Meridian
with all its depots, storehouses, hotels, arsenals, hospitals,
offices, railroads and cantonments and fine homes no longer
exists." The Yankees stripped every home of quilts, blankets,
and clothes before they destroyed everything. The destruction
was fearsome, and Sherman took pleasure in his reports as he
listed the results: 53 bridges, 19 locomotives, 28 railcars, 55
miles of tracks in each direction. "We made a swath of
destruction 50 miles wide across the entire state of Mississippi
which will take generations to forget. We bring 500 prisoners
and about 10 miles of Negroes straggling behind."

After the fighting across Alabama up into Tennessee, Sherman
then turned his attention to Georgia. After four months of
fighting and 130 miles, he was looking as a time for rest and
recovery in the city of Atlanta. Gaining Atlanta with so little
effort gave Sherman a new boldness and solidified his plan of
a march to the sea. (An interesting side note: Sherman's
personal escort on the march was the 1st Alabama Cavalry
Regiment, a unit made up entirely of Alabama men who
remained loyal to the Union.) After capturing Atlanta,
Sherman decided that it would be more easily defended if the
civilians were evacuated, so Sherman informed all residents
that they had to leave. The Mayor and City Council protested,

saying the results of an order to evacuate would be appalling and heartrending. Sherman replied that the Confederacy had begun this conflict and was responsible for all bloodshed. "You cannot qualify war in harsher terms than I will," he told the Mayor. "War is cruelty and you cannot refine it; and those who brought war into our country deserve all the curses and maledictions a people can pour out. One may as well appeal against the thunderstorm as against these terrible hardships of war. They are inevitable, and the only way the people of Atlanta can hope once more to live in peace is to stop this war."

As Sherman contemplated his next move, he announced to his men that he had the perfect plan. He could not afford to stay on the defensive. Far better was to take the offensive and confound the enemy. He would march his army across Georgia, all the way to Savannah on to the Atlantic coast. Nothing would more demoralize the Confederates than to find a federal army cutting a swath across the heartland, using lessons learned in Mississippi, living off the inhabitants and spreading terror and destruction across the 275 miles to the sea. After wasting time and energy fighting back and forth with southern Gen. Hood for a while, Sherman got Gen. Grant and Pres. Lincoln to agree to start his campaign. But first, they would destroy anything and everything in the city that could be of use to the South. Knowing the South would re-occupy as soon as they left, they began by demolishing railroad stations, warehouses, and all factories, smashing brick and stone buildings level with the ground. Then they put

Atlanta to the torch. Flames spread quickly through the
industrial district. Then the wind caught up and "immense
and raging flames lighted up the whole heavens. Huge waves
of flame spread in all directions into the fine homes of the
residential areas. Sherman's plan was of destruction, to teach
the South the futility of war, and to grind the South under the
heel of the Union.

As Sherman's troops marched out of the burning city, they
were sure that Atlanta was ruined, yet two weeks later a
newspaper was published. Atlanta was battered, but far from
dead. Sherman continued to ravage the Georgia countryside,
sending patrols out to gather food and supplies from the
people, taking cows, sheep, goats, pigs, chickens, mules,
horses, and any and all supplies. Fighting battles, meeting
some resistance, but always winning, Sherman laid waste to
Georgia, arriving at Savannah on December 17. Sherman sent
a message to the people of Savannah demanding surrender
and a threat of terrible retribution if the city did not. Sherman
said, "If you do not accept my terms, I shall then feel justified
in resorting to the harshest measures, and will make little
effort to restrain my army, already burning to avenge the
national wrong which they attach to Savannah and other large
cities which have been so prominent in dragging our country
into civil war."

The next morning the mayor, Richard Dennis Arnold, rode
out with some aldermen and ladies of the city to offer a
proposition. The city would surrender and offer no resistance

in exchange for a promise to protect the citizens and property. Gen. Geary, on Sherman's advice, accepted the city, and Savannah peacefully surrendered.

Sherman and his forces destroyed so much more than military targets. He disrupted the South's economy and so much civilian property and civilian lives and infrastructure that to this day the name of General Sherman is reviled. Making war on the women and children of the South was and is not forgotten.

SOUTHERN WRITING 101
(Or, how NOT to write about the South)

Writers have attempted to define the American South for generations, and continued efforts to interpret the southern mind have proved to be both a maddening and enlightening experience. For some interpreters of southern history, the ills of our region are easily diagnosed and the picture is far too clear. Southern institutions are peculiar and strange, much too different from New York or Boston to identify with; the land is lurid and backwards, and the inhabitants are eccentric, racist, ignorant and neo-confederates.

This perception of a mystical and strange South is due in part to the popularity of notable works of FICTION by celebrated authors such as William Faulkner, Tennessee Williams, Flannery O'Connor, Erskine Caldwell, Harry Crews, James Dickey, Barry Hannah, Larry Brown, Eudora Welty, Kathryn Stockett, and most recently Gregg Isles, who postulates that everyone in Natchez, Mississippi was or is a member of the Ku Klux Klan, had interracial romances, and was guilty of having knowledge of horrible crimes committed by white citizens.

These writers have penned literary masterpieces that portray the anguished, the Gothic, and the grotesque South. Readers enjoy creative and ingenious stories which reflect the dark themes of human nature as well as the triumphs of human spirit. The South continues to provide writers with colorful characters, enduring themes and ideal settings: the perfect ingredients for tall tales and stirring fiction. Literary critics (who have never been south of Washington DC) praise books that reinforce deeply rooted perceptions of the South, and this creates a strong impression on those who have never visited the South. While many fictional accounts are somewhat believable and contain elements of truth, readers would find that authentic history is even more fascinating and revealing.

Northern writers contend that the South is different and to an extent this is true, but for reasons that are not always understood. Their primary focus is often on themes that involve race, gender, repression and intolerance, ignorance and greed, (traits shared by all parts of the world) yet there are other topics capable of providing valuable and interesting insight if adequately and dispassionately studied. It is easy to forget that

the South endured terrible ordeals not shared by the rest of the nation: military defeat, grinding federal occupation, loss of land and fortunes, and a reconstruction program that lasted for years and was a dismal failure. The aftermath of these tragic episodes left the South with the curse of sustained poverty that has plagued the South for generations.

These historic experiences have impacted the behavior, mindset, and perspective of each generation since.

It is unfortunate that modern critics and writers do not take the time to study southern history in depth or to investigate the viewpoints of Southerners (other than minority groups).

Too often authors rely on their own preconceived notions and northern myopia that reinforce the common northern stereotypes and present a microscopic view of the true history of the South. This is disappointing because the unfortunate reader must endure, once again, additional helpings of well-worn material plus redundant and spiteful opinion, all sold as profound historical insight, and of course the "mind of the South" remains murky and hard to understand.

In recent years, Southerners have become more vocal in expressing their concerns about the lack of balance in news, books, TV, and movies, especially historical presentations, and there is validity to these concerns. Writers of nonfiction publications and producers of TV programs seldom or never include Southern interpretations in any of their work.

For example, Ken Burns, the creator of the epic PBS series "The Civil War" actually bristles when questioned about the fairness and balance of his documentary. Many Americans believe the series was one-sided, and some writers have called it the "New England" version of the war. National writers and reporters fill the magazines and papers such as the Wall Street Journal with quotes and statements from people who are questionable at best, as typical representatives of all things Southern. (I suppose that if a fringe element of any group is quoted long enough and often enough, sensational news will be generated and unknowing audiences will be titillated.) Also, it is interesting to observe how the people of the South, especially working-class white people, are depicted in political

cartoons and sensational news articles: always the laughing
stock - dull, ignorant, poor grammar, racist, unkempt,
unlettered! (The only segment of the population that the PC
police allow anyone to ridicule is a white Southerner.) This
type of journalism will win awards for writers and publishers
and bring forth speaking invitations and Sunday morning TV
appearances for the authors, but the message being delivered
is elitist and very negative and can only be interpreted as
disdain for all things and all people Southern!

Recently the July-August, 2014, issue of the Smithsonian
Magazine presented a long article by Paul Theroux, an alleged
world traveler, and native of Massachusetts and Hawaii. 31 of
the 140 total pages in the slick-paper magazine were devoted
to his trip south, in which he discovered the very "Soul of the
South." He spent a couple of days in South Carolina, several
days in Alabama and Arkansas, sparing four or five pages to
each state, and then he devoted the bulk of the article (14
pages) to the ills and history of the civil rights movement in
the state of Mississippi, decrying the fact that Mississippi has
gun shows and Bible verses on signs nailed to trees beside the
road. He perceived these verses as death threats. (Repent;
Faith without works is dead; Strive to enter at the straight
gate.) I guess being from Massachusetts, Bible verses would
seem strange or out of place in his life. Most of the article
consisted of an interview with Blues great B.B. King's first
wife (?) and minority group members. He made a flying trip
through Oxford to see the William Faulkner home Rowan
Oaks, then flew back to Massachusetts having captured the

"very heart and soul of the South." How about Tennessee, Louisiana, Georgia, Florida, and North Carolina: are they not Southern? This guy was most likely paid a large amount of money to write this trite, hatchet job on the South.

Let's say I, a native and resident of Mississippi, flew into Detroit, Monday morning. I spend the day touring the thousands of abandoned, burned-out homes which line street after street, then the rusting, abandoned factories where the unions forced manufacturing out of business with their outrageous demands. I take a police escort into the slums to see the gangs of youths, fifth generation of welfare, all hanging out buying and selling drugs and shooting and killing each other. Then I go down by the Court House where the minority group mayor was convicted and sent to prison for stealing millions, and where the biggest bankruptcy of a city in the USA was taking place. The next day I fly up to North Michigan, hire a guide, and in the vast forest I shoot a moose, taking a picture of the head of the moose.

I then fly home and write an article for a well-known magazine, having captured the very "Heart, Soul and Essence" of Michigan and the North!

SOME INTERESTING FACTS ABOUT OUR STATE

INFO COURTESY FARM BUREAU OF MISSISSIPPI

SUBMITTED BY David H. McBRIDE

Mississippi is in the top 20 in the production of 15 important agricultural commodities.

No. 1 in Catfish

No. 3 in Pulpwood

No. 3 in Sweet Potatoes

No. 5 in Broilers

No. 6 in Cotton

No   6 in Cottonseed

No. 6 in Rice

No   7 in Peanuts

No. 9 in Blueberries

No. 9 in Pecans (That is Puh-Kahns to Southerners)

No. 10 in Grain Sorghum

No. 12 in Soybeans

No. 17 in Eggs

No. 17 in Pigs and Hogs

There are 42,300 Farms in Mississippi valued at $23.9 Billion.

11.2 million acres of land farmed in Mississippi.

Average Farm size is 264 acres

Mississippi has 19,700,000 acres of Forest land with 125,000 different landowners. $1.17 Billion value of production last year

736,000,000 broilers produced last year.

1,478 farms.

$2.50 billion value of production last year.

For those who have always wondered? Sweet Potatoes and Yams are not the same thing. They are not even first cousins, no kin at all.

Different species totally.

Sweet Potatoes were native to the New World, and unknown till The Spaniards took them from South America, across the Pacific Ocean, to the Philippine islands then to China, China is the World's largest grower and consumer of Sweet potatoes.

SOME OLD SAYINGS
For "Good Ole Boys & Girls"

(NOTE: I don't remember where/when I heard or read these sayings. They are stuck in my memory bank so I will share them. If anyone remembers where they came from or WHO said them, please feel free to contact me and I will give proper credit to whoever! Some may be original or I may have paraphrased them over the years. I like them!)

- A man may have his will but a woman will have her way!
- The amount of sleep required by the average person is "just five minutes more."
- A "liberal" is a man with both feet firmly planted in the air.
- Old age will not last very long.
- The principal objection to old age is "There's no future in it."
- A man who sees both sides of the issue is a man who sees absolutely nothing at all.
- Psychology: A blind man in a dark room looking for a black hat, which is not there.
- The object of psychology is to give us a totally different idea of anything we know for a fact.
- Sin has been made out to be a thing of the past, people are no longer sinful, they are only "misunderstood or frightened, under privileged, immature or mentally ill."

- Politics is perhaps the only profession for which no thought or any preparation is deemed necessary.
- Little things seem to have much effect on little minds.
- We should never really grow up, we should only learn how to act in public.
- Since light travels faster than sound, some people appear bright, until you hear them speak.
- Yes, you are free to choose but you are not free from the consequences of your choice.
- When you judge others you do not define them. You define yourself.
- Your beliefs do not make you a better person, your actions do.
- Repeating a lie does not make it the truth, only accepted.
- If ethics and economics clash, the bottom line will rule.
- There is someone for everyone and the person for you may be just a psychiatrist.

PEOPLE I'D LIKE TO MEET & HAVE A TALK WITH

1. The person who thinks folks in the USA would like to buy their insurance from a little green lizard that speaks with a bad Aussie or British accent.
2. The person who crossed a tomato with a ball of paper mache to create a vegetable that looks like a tomato, yet tastes like a wad of cardboard.
3. The person who thinks Americans want to hear OUR news read by a person with a British accent, and who seems to sneer at all we hold dear!
4. The person who thinks it is important to interrupt a program I am watching to comment on some rain storm 150 miles away, and blab about it for 10 minutes til I've missed the end of my show.
5. The person who turns up the volume on all TV commercials.
6. The person (maybe the same one) who ensures that all TV commercials air at the same time, so you can't change the channels to check what's happening on another channel.

A BRIEF HISTORY OF THE NATIVE AMERICANS OF THE SOUTHEAST
A Presentation

Introduction

History, it has been said many times, is written by the winners, and our records and history books have proven this for many generations. Though this subject has been worked and re-worked in books, movies, plays, and television, the Native Americans remain the least understood and the most misunderstood of all. The fact that millions of people were living on this continent in 1492 has been largely ignored by our history books. We have been conditioned to think of the Indians greeting English Settlers at East Coast settlements. Yet, for nearly two hundred years, Spanish Explorers had crossed the southern and western part of the United States countless times. In the southeastern region, the native peoples inhabited a civilization, highly developed, over thousands of years, culminating the Mississippian mound-building culture.

As De Soto looted and killed his way across the area, he was unaware that he and his men would be the last Europeans to see the great chiefdoms of the mound-building cultures. By the time the French and English explorers and settlers came in around 1700, the entire area was a scene of desolation. Scoured by wave after wave of diseases brought by the Spanish and their African slaves, sacred mounds had long since fallen into despair with former cities and trading sites forgotten. The mound-builders' legacy endured on in tribal tradition and creation myths.

Because of the broad scope and the short length of this history, it has been necessary to generalize about people who were no more uniform, or a single people than their European counterparts.

It is very apparent that many important aspects of their history are obscure, and probably lost forever.

Because of the vast scope of subject matter, this brief history will deal only with the southeastern quadrant of the United States and the area of the Gulf of Mexico. Any reader desiring more detail on any related subject is invited to contact the writer. Other related areas may include, but are not limited to, religion, tribes, social structure, languages, geographic location, food, trading routes, highways, early contact, cities, etc.

macb@aol.com

Chapter I

Everyone has heard the story of how in fourteen hundred and ninety-two, Columbus sailed the ocean blue, and found a new land and found new people. The further truth is, however, that when the white man of Spain, with Columbus as their leader, shattered the isolated world of the native peoples of North America, it set in motion a chain of events that is still reverberating in our world today. Changes that affected our diet, our various cultures, and our very way of life. From the first contact with these people some four hundred years ago, a series of burning questions had arisen: Who are these people? Who were these people? Where did they come from? How did they get here? At some unknown time and place, after the development of *Homosapiens sapiens*, the forebears of the American Indians entered into the still untouched New World. The where and when of that entrance has excited a great deal of guesswork.

There has been great speculation that the Indians were displaced Greeks, Phoenicians, Romans, Chinese, Welsh, Irish, or descendants of the ten lost tribes of Israel. Or of having made their way hither via the lost continent of Atlantis, or lost continent of Mu, or both. Modern science has shown that the American Indians are far more ancient than any of these candidates. Finds have been made proving the presence of Man in America, at the time of such Ice Age big game as camels, mammoths, the giant sound sloth, and primitive horses. In other words, during the last of the Pleistocene glaciers, the last great ice age that drew to a close over ten thousand years ago. With recent data, event that remote date is pushed further and further into the past.

Researchers recently announced that humans may have entered the New World as far back as thirty, even thirty-eight thousand years ago. The archeologist who led the team that made these revolutionizing finds in a New Mexico cave on the grounds of Fort Bliss, have pronounced them incontrovertible evidence of the presence of humans before the usually cited date of twelve thousand years ago. While several claims of comparatively old or even older finds have been made, none have offered both indisputable evidence of human presence and secure dating.

Experts in this long simmering controversy of just when the ancient Indians' ancestors crossed into North America, said the new discovery may come closer than ever to providing the decisive combination of data. Scientists heard a report at the annual meeting of the American Association for the Advancement of Science which said that most of the signs of human presence are what appear to be human palm and fingerprints on clay found in a twenty-eight thousand year old layer and a number of hearths in various layers going back as far as thirty-eight thousand years ago. In addition, many of them were found to be ringed with fire-cracked stones and still holding charred logs up to eight inches in diameter. The prints, which have been identified as human by police forensic scientists, were on clay, shaped to serve as a fire pit and then hardened by the fire.

This report was made by Richard S. McNeish, of the Andover Foundation for Archeological Research in Massachusetts. McNeish being one of the county's best known specialists on the peopling of the New World, had previously found sites in Central and South America that strongly suggested an early human presence. "But this is the one that will finish off the skeptics," he said. The shallow cave contains twenty-five distinct layers that had been dated by radiocarbon method, and in some cases confirmed by a newer method, thermoluminescience. McNeish reported that in addition to the hearths, many layers contained the bones of tapirs, horses, llamas, giant bison and many species that are now extinct.

Recently digging in a cave near the Amazon River in Brazil, archeologists have found rock paintings and other traces of what may have been one of the earliest cultures in the South American region. The discovery could revise thinking and will stir more controversy about the lives and migration of the first Americans. These excavations yielded evidence that the ancient people who regularly camped in this cave, led lived very distinct from the big game hunters who roamed the hills and plains of western North America at the same time, which is dated to about eleven thousand years ago. These people of the Amazon lived off the fruits and nuts and small game of the forest and they took fish from the river. Their paintings on the cave walls are thought to be the earliest reliable dated examples of art found in the Americas.

These findings, being reported today in the *Journal of Science*, challenged the widely held assumption that the earliest Americans were primarily specialized big game hunters who lived in open, temperate country, and could not have sustained a culture in the humid tropics where large game is scarce. They had supposedly migrated across the Bering Straits from Asia, settled in North America, then gradually moved into South America, continuing as a hunting society and living in the highlands. These hunters were presumed to be the forerunners of cultures in South America. This research in the Amazon seems to confirm earlier evidence that the spread of the paleo-Indians through the Americas was much more complex and widespread than the theories can explain.

The *New York Times* has recently reported that anthropologists at Nevada State Museum had unearthed the oldest known mummy. And they had found it right on their own shelves. The mummy known as the Spirit Cave Man had been found in a Nevada cave in the 1940's. but advanced in dating had only recently allowed scientists to determine that the remains they thought had dated back to two thousand years were, in fact, more than nine thousand, four hundred years old. The mummy's great age and excellent state of preservation will provide critical new information on what life was like here at the end of the Ice Age, including a previously unsuspected sophisticated level of textile weaving, and a clue as to the identity of the continent's earliest settlers. Anthropologists are delighted, because they say, "We anticipate this will bear greatly on what we know about the peopling of the New World."

The Spirit Cave Man will provide a wealth of information about the times in which he lived. The fish bones in his mummified intestines will tell much about his diet. He was wearing moccasins and wrapped in shroud woven from marsh plants. It is woven so neatly that it would indicated that the peoples of that era were using looms. The mummy is expected to undergo extensive testing, including DNA analysis which will help to determine his genetic makeup and offer more about the environment of the Great Basin which overs Nevada and Utah.

The Spirit Cave Man's great age is surpassed by mummified remains more than ten thousand years old that have been found in South America. And there are skeletal remains in North America that are much older. But he is far older than the famous Ice Man Mummy discovered in the Alps in 1991 which is only five thousand years old. The discovery that he is so much older than previously suspected shows that there may be many hidden treasures that have yet to come to light as museums examine their collections. Such evidence may reveal that we are steadily being blown towards a more distant dawn of the age of Man in North and South America than was previously believed.

One eminent geographer concludes that the basic peopling of the Americas may have occurred before the primordial bloodstream of man became mingled. Blood group studies of living Indians have recorded the purest type A groups in the world, as well as the only known populations entirely lacking A. The purest O groups are also found among Indians, as well as the purest B groups.

One thing is obvious, the American Indians can claim direct descent from these early people of fifteen, twenty, thirty and forty thousand years ago. They are, by far, the oldest known race on the face of the earth. There is no evidence of an identifiable appearance of any other such modern races. There is no identification of Mongolian, White or Negro race until much later. Time is the tonic cord in the story of the Indians. With this sort of antiquity, it is clear that the first Indians must have arrived here long before the rest of the races of the world began their rise.

All the unanswered questions, and there are a great many, lend fuel to many speculations. Recently, a new unanswered question has emerged. Botanical evidence shows the New World cotton is a cross between Asiatic cotton and American wild cotton. If so, it would appear that the Asiatic plant must have been brought across the Pacific by the hand of man. It is generally agreed that no one could have walked around with it by way of the Bering Strait. Fancy can play some pretty fine games with possible trans-Pacific communication at such a remote period. Bottle gourds, also common to Asia, are found with some of these early appearances of New World cotton. The early appearance of cotton in extremely primitive sites in Northern Peruvian coasts produces carbon fourteen dates of about six thousand years old.

An early date of considerable interest comes from the Great Lakes area in and around Wisconsin, where the people of the old copper culture made lance points, some of them socketed, and many ornamental trinkets. A profusion of other articles from the copper native to this region. Till very recently this culture was thought to date back twelve to fifteen hundred years ago. And it was amazing to find such a well-developed copper industry so early as a leading archeologist wrote as recently as 1949. Since then, carbon fourteen tests and other evidence has dated this copper culture back to somewhere between seven and nine thousand years ago. This indicated a very early time for the use of metal, anywhere in the world.

What is known and understood today, is that the land from one end of the Americas to the other including Canada, United States, Mexico, Central America, and all of South

America, was once inhabited and populated with Indians. These communities stretched from the Atlantic to the Pacific, from the Arctic to the border and bottom of South America including Mexico and Caribbean. Many of these cities and communities dated back far before the time of the Roman Empire. This was a continent of populated with as many as forty million people. Some of them were nomadic, but most of them were permanently settled in communities that ranged in size from isolated villages to cities as large and sophisticated as any in the world. Every part of the land, and all of the natural world within it was occupied by these native peoples.

Not unlike today, the most dense populations were along the coastlines and the major rivers, as well as around the Great Lakes. There were also heavily populated areas in Mexico, Florida, the Caribbean Islands, and California. There were over six hundred distinct languages spoken by the different communities. There were bands of nomads, there were permanent villages, there were cities, and major and minor chiefdoms that made up the vast North American continent. There were Indian kings and prophets, architects, sculptors and poets, mathematicians and doctors. Land and water trade networks interconnected the continent, spreading various commodities and ideas.

In medicine, sports, military service, dance, religion and art, and in a dozen other fields, Indians could dream of personal accomplishments. Not unlike today, all of these possibilities existed in a different way in each nation. Traditions, environment, different forms of government all played a role in giving these nations their identity and diversity, and directing them along their individual paths. Some were committed by a thousand years of tradition to perfecting unchanging ways of life. Others built armies, and military empires.

From the very first arrival of the Europeans in the Western Hemisphere, the Whites marveled at what they saw, and wondered where it all came from. "Who were these people? Who are these people?" they asked. And from whence did they originate? This question tantalized generations of scholars and scientists. Some have spent lifetimes trying to prove point A or point B. Trying to prove that Indians were descendants of sea-faring Phoenicians, or Pyramid-building Egyptians, or descendants of the Lost Tribes of Israel. The question of their origin will never be completely solved until we excavated more of the land of the continents of North and South America.

Chapter II

As Columbus landed at the Bahaman Islands in
October of 1492, then sailed along the verdant coast of Cuba
and Hispanola, which is present day Haiti and the Dominican
Republic, he and his bearded and heavily armored Spaniards
made frequent landings among the villages of the Arawak
speaking peoples. Lost and thinking he was in the East Indies
of Asia, Columbus referred to these inhabitants as Los Indos,
or, the Indians, thus fastening the name on the population of
all the indigenous nations of the Western Hemisphere. This
was a dramatic moment of first contact between two worlds.
Both the Indians and the Europeans were filled with wonder
about each other. To Columbus, the Indians were artless and
generous with what they had. He related in one of his journals
that they were, "to such a degree, that no one would believe
but he who has seen it. Of anything they have, if he ask for it,
they never say no, but do rather invite the person to accept it
and show lovingness though they would give their heart." But
at the same time, Columbus made note of what he understood
of what the Indians were thinking, "They believe that I and
my ships and crew came from the ski. And with such an
opinion have received me at every place."

The awe and the innocence of the Arawaks worked to
Columbus' benefit. Wherever he landed he proclaimed
possession of the Indians' land and resources for Spain, then
turn to his major objective of the expedition: the subjugation
and forced conversion of people to Christianity, and a search
for gold and anything else that would enrich the Spanish
monarchs and himself. Two days after he had landed and
noted how generous the Indians were, he wrote, "These

people are unskilled in arms. With fifty men they could all be subjected and made to do what we wish." His actions soon followed his words. "As soon as I arrived in the Indies," he wrote, "the first of them I found, I took some of them by force by the intent they should learn to give me information there was in these parts." This was a harbinger of what was to come.

In 1492, millions of Arawak Indians were living in the islands of the Caribbean. Estimates vary widely, but most recently, archeologists suggest that the pre-Columbian population of Hispaniola alone, may have been as high as seven or eight million. Originally, the Arawaks had come from South America, emigrating from island to island in large canoes at probably around 500 BC, displacing earlier hunting and gathering known as Sibones. By the time of Columbus, the Sibones were concentrated in only a small area of Cuba and Haiti, and were soon extinct.

About a century before the arrival of the Spaniards, the Arawak in turn, had come under pressure from a new wave of migrants from South America; aggressive, war-like Carib Indians who terrorized the Arawaks and forced them out of the lesser Antilles to the islands farther north. Columbus did not meet any Caribs during his voyages, but from the Arawaks, he understood that these were fearsome enemies, and that these people reportedly ate the flesh of their captives. On his later voyages, Columbus became familiar with the Caribs, but there was never any credible evidence from any white man that the Caribs ate human flesh. Nevertheless, from their name, which was sometimes pronounced, "cannibal," by Columbus' reference to them from his first voyage, the world was given the dreaded word Cannibal.

The Arawaks were both horticulturists and expert boat builders and navigators. And over a two thousand year period, they had developed a complex agricultural and trading society, living very comfortably in their islands and the waters of the surrounding seas. Navigating in large, ocean-going canoes, some capable of carrying as many as a hundred and fifty men, the Arawaks traveled between islands, even to distant mainland villages in Florida, Meseo-America and Central and South America. Their crafts went forth laden with traders and their goods; feathers, gold, pottery, cotton thread fabric, parrots, fruits and other foods. Trade was frequent and common between the islands of the Caribbean and Florida coastal regions.

The Spaniard immediately assumed a posture of human and cultural superiority over the Indians. A Euro-centric stance that, in time, other European imperial powers would adopt, and bequeathed the consequences of such to generations of non-Indians throughout all of the Americas. From the very beginning of contact between the islanders and the Spaniards, the monumental differences in their cultures, and the way in which they viewed each other's worlds, created misunderstandings that would draw tragic consequence for the Indians. One such gross misunderstanding occurred by the premise that Columbus espoused when he reported, "I believe they could very easily become Christians, for it seemed to me that they had no religion." Actually, the Arawaks possessed a rich spiritual life inherited from centuries of ancestors.

From his first voyage, Columbus took back to his king, six slaves that he had captured to show off upon his return to Spain. "They are fit to be ordered about and made to work, to sow and to do all else that may be needed," he noted in his letter. Adding darkly, that among the wealth he could ship from these lands to add to the wealth of the sovereigns, were the Indian slaves, "as many as they shall order."

On his second voyage, Columbus had seventeen ships, twelve hundred colonists and thirty-four horses, (the first in the Western hemisphere since the disappearance of the ice age horses). Columbus returned in November of 1493, and on his way to Hispaniola, he stopped briefly on the island now known as St. Croix. There, without provocation, his expedition attacked Indian men and women in a canoe, cutting off the heads of the men with an ax and taking the other Indians captive on board the ship, in order to send back to Spain as slaved. It is the first recorded incident of a killing of an Indian by the Spaniards and reflects the arrogance and cruelty with which the Europeans, led by Columbus himself would no deal with the natives.

Between 1495 and 1496, epidemics of European diseases against which the island Indians had no defense, began to sweep away great members of them. Still the Spaniards demanded that the Indians work and supply the white men with food. The suffering of the Indians became so intense, that natives by the thousands took their own lives. "Many went into the woods," wrote Benzoni, a critic of the Spanish cruelties, "and hanged themselves after having killed their children. Saying that was far better than for them to die miserably." Some thousands threw themselves off cliffs and high precipieces to their deaths and others threw themselves into the sea. By 1502, only a few of the Arawaks, fighting for their freedom remained in the mountainous regions. By 1520, only two hundred Indians remained alive on the entire island of Hispanola. By 1552, there were none alive anywhere.

Northwest of the Arawaks and Caribs of the West Indies, in the southern peninsula and on the mainland, there was another proud and determined nation, that of the Calusa, who had fought hard against the Spaniards. Possessing one of the most unusual civilizations in North America, the Calusa built their capitol city, known as Calos, on a huge shell mound of the peninsula's southwest coast in the area San Carlos Bay, which is near present day Ft. Meyers, FL.

Few places on earth could have been more benign or beautiful that southern Florida. In its coastal waters and meadows there was an abundance of food that Indian populations and their cultures arose and flourished without the development of agriculture. The Calusa were maritime oriented, but did much more than just fish; they farmed the sea. They created systems of lagoons for oyster beds and stone holding pens for sea turtles, mullet and other fish that were in great abundance.

Centuries before the arrival of the Europeans, the Calusa extended their influence across southern Florida, the Atlantic coast and Lake Oceechobee, which they called, Miami, in a trade and communication network that stretched for hundreds of miles through the swamps and interior hammocks. In time, they dominated all the tribes of the southern part of the Florida peninsula, and held sway over some fifty tributary towns. In addition, the Calusa traders, experienced in long distance sea travel, journeyed in canoes. These were large, shovel nosed double canoes that lashed together, resembling catamarans, and equipped with a sail, could accommodate fifty men. The Indians visited coastal towns along the islands of the Florida Keys, the Bahamas and Cuba.

From his state house at Calos, where he could entertain two thousand guests, the Calusa king ruled with authority, commanding not only a standing army, but the operation of a variety of public works. The Calusa people also built islands. Many Calusa towns rose from the coastal waters on these large, man-made islands. The grandeur of the ceremonial center on San Marco was legendary and covered nearly fifty acres.

The Calusas had heard of the Spaniards and their ships, as early as the time of Columbus, from the Indian traders and canoes that had crossed from the islands to the mainland, bringing the news. When the ships of bearded strangers began to appear off the Florida coast, those reports of the white man had become real. Here and there, the ships stopped, and armed groups of slave-catching Spaniards came ashore kidnapping Indians to take back to sell as laborers to the Caribbean Island landholders. Word of the white man's aggressiveness and evil spread from town to town among the Calusas, where a revered and aged chief, later known to the Spaniards as Carlos, lived in the nation's capital. Believing that something had thrown their world out of balance, sending this new, threatening force against them, Carlos and his people regarded the Spaniards not as gods, but as enemies to be fought.

MOUND COMPLEX, MOUNDVILLE, AL

TYPICAL OF SHAPE

"I have learned who you Spanish are. You are vagabonds, who wander from place to place, gaining your livelihood by robbing, sacking and killing people who have given you no offense."

– Florida Chief 1539

"When white people win a battle, it is a 'great victory'. When they lose a battle, it becomes a 'massacre'."

-- Chiksika-Shawnee

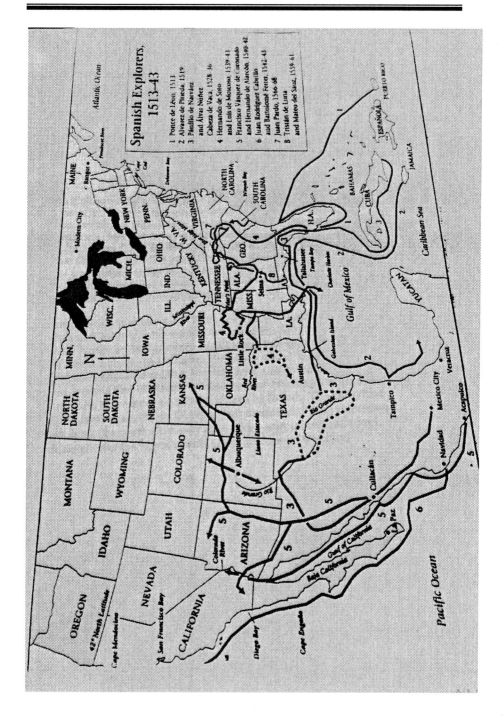

FRANCISCO DE CHICORA

While the Calusa were defending their Florida beaches against Ponce de Leon, inhabitants of the Carolina coast had a brush with other marauding Spaniards. In the summer of 1521, Lucas Vasquez de Ayllon, a major landholder on the island of Hispaniola, sent agents up the Atlantic seaboard looking for slaves to work his sugar plantations. They landed along the South Santee River, in an area the Spanish called Chicora. Here the people knew nothing yet of Spanish motives. Eager to view the wonderful floating islands on which the foreigners had arrived, a group of natives trustingly boarded one of the ships-and the captain promptly set sale for Hispaniola with about 60 kidnapped slaves.

Many died of sickness on the way. But one became a useful ally of the Spanish: Francisco de Chicora, as his captors dubbed him, learned their language and journeyed with Ayllon to Spain, where his glowing description helped convince the authorities to found a colony in Chicora. Francisco sailed back to his home waters with the Spanish expedition; then, almost as soon as the ships dropped anchor in 1526, he escaped and obviously wasted no time warning his people. When Ayllon began to explore, there were no inhabitants to be found. The chagrined Spaniard tried again farther south, in Georgia, but disease and near starvation drove his followers from the coast after only six weeks-and spared the people of Chicora and their neighbors the worst effects of the European invasion.

De Soto and his men encountered remnants of the great
Mississippian cultures that had flourished in the Southeast for
hundreds of years. Many still consisted of politically and
religiously centralized chiefdoms ruled by priests, nobles, and
paramount chiefs. The long structure in the center of this De
Bry engraving of a Timucuan town in Florida was a "town
hall" or statehouse, for the chief and his councilors and served
also for ceremonies and community meetings. It was
surrounded by the dwellings of the villagers and by a palisade
for protection from enemies.

Chapter III

The explorer, Ponce de Leon became the first known European to be driven off by the Caloosa. De Leon had accompanied Columbus to the West Indies on his second voyage in 1493. And as a leader in the suppression of the Indians on Hispanola, he had then conquered Puerto Rico, enslaving the Indians and becoming rich as a slave trader. In 1512 he received royal permission of explore to the north and he sailed the next year. History says he was in search of a spring on an island called Bimini, which the Indians had assured him would restore a man's youth. But it is more likely he was bent on finding a new source of slaves. He failed to find the fountain of youth, but did officially reveal to the Old World the presence of the land he reached in 1513, which he named Pascal Florida, after the Eastertime Feast of Flowers in April season. This first landing was on the Atlantic coast of the peninsula and in the domains of the Temuca and Ais Indians. Both tribes regarded him as a slave trader and after a few fierce skirmishes, drove him off, although he did manage to kidnap a few Indians.

In 1521, Ponce de Leon, although sixty years old, appeared again, this time leading two hundred settlers intent on establishing a colony in Carlos' territory. The Spanish settlers managed to land and erect a temporary settlement before a large force of Calusas attached them. Although the settlers' horses and forearms aided them, the Indians, fighting with darts and arrows, inflicted heavy losses on the Europeans and seriously wounded Ponce in the thigh. The injured explorer gave up a second time with the survivors of his failed colony and sailed for Havana, where he soon died from his inflected arrow wound.

In 1519, Alvarez de Pinata sailed from the west coast of Florida to the east coast of Mexico. With his four ships and four hundred men sailing along the north coast area, he stayed forty days at the mouth of a river in large bay that was probably Mobile, or Pensacola Bay. Pinata left some of his men behind and was joined by another expedition led by Diego de Carmega. This expedition fought constantly with the Indians and traveled back and forth across the Gulf coast area for two years and produced a map in 1519, which is a fairly accurate account of Gulf coastline.

In 1528, Panfilio de Navarez sailed across the Gulf coast area with five ships and six hundred men. He explored the coast all the way from the edge of Mexico all around the coastline including the Mississippi River and the islands around the coast of Florida. He explored intensively the inland area around Tallahassee, and then left the mainland in early 1529 at the coast near Mobile.

In 1539, there awaited near the shore of Tampa, Florida, the man who would do more towards the destruction of the nations of Indians peoples of the southeastern region of the United States than any other, Hernando DeSoto. DeSoto, who was Francisco Pizarro's sternest lieutenant in the destruction of the Incan empire in Peru, set out to find more treasures of gold hidden among the undiscovered Indians nations of the mainland. This time he had a license from the Spanish king to conquer, pacify and people what is now the southeast portion of the United States. He began by landing above the Calusas' territory on Florida's west coast with an army of six hundred soldiers, one hundred servants, two hundred and fifty horses, herds of pack animals, a large herd of swine and a pack of attack dogs; terrifying greyhounds which he paid the wages of soldiers.

DeSoto entered the lush and fertile country, the wooded mountains and green valleys and swampy bottoms of the southeaster chiefdoms. For four years, throughout this ancient world from Florida to Texas, DeSoto and his expedition cut a wide path of destruction, unparalleled in the annals of explorative history. First they marched through the densely populated areas of Florida, the lands to strong chiefdoms, entering one town after another, plundering their foodstores and valuables. Threatening torture and death to those who resisted, they seized men and women, commoners and members of ruling classes. They took them as burden bearers, clapping them in great iron collars connected by chains. Stories of the barbarism of the Spaniards spread among the Indians and some of their chiefs managed to get some of their people out of the way. Winding his way through Georgia and the Carolinas, he employed the usual tactics of capturing the local chief, holding him or her until the army had passed through, forcing the members of the first village to transport his goods and arms on to the next, and using the women for sexual rewards for his men.

Near Montgomery, Alabama, in the fall of 1540, DeSoto's luck with the natives ran out. At Mobile, the Indians under their chief, Tuscaloosa, took a stand. Indian losses ranged from a ow estimate of three thousand to a high of eleven thousand. DeSoto lost 30 to 60 men, twelve horses and, worst of all, most of his baggage. One of the most perplexing questions that arose on this journey was a result of the loss of their flour, which they carried. Could the communion Eucharist be made of maize? After much discussion, the priest decided it could not, so there would be no communion for the men.

DeSoto's four thousand mile journey took him four years and took him through ten states, and on July 18, 1543, after four disastrous years, the expedition of DeSoto mercifully came to an end. Unfortunately, the consequences on the Indian nations of the southeast were permanent and tragic.

Sixteen years later, another Spaniard, Tristan de Luna, with five hundred soldiers and a thousand colonists, sailed along the Pensacola coast of west Florida, the land of the Coosa chiefdoms. They were veterans of DeSoto's journey and kept alive the tales of a verdant province where a day's travel would take a man through a dozen towns where food was abundant. Luna had been sent forth to establish a colony and to make use of the legendary wealth of the Coosa to supply the settlements of the Spanish along the Atlantic coast. But as they moved inland those that had been there with DeSoto did not find the land they remembered. The few towns they saw were small and poor. In one of them, the remnant of a thriving Coosa town, a woman told a Spaniard, "Our town had once been great. But the Spaniards came, and now it's the way it is. We have all died."

The capitol of Coosa was even a greater shock. Instead of five hundred houses, there were only fifty. The great temple mound stood in decay. Cornfields were overgrown and abandoned. No chief greeted them, no retinues of men in feathered headdresses lined the roadways. The people were

all gone. A sick Spanish slave left by DeSoto in the care of a
young Coosa chief, had spread an epidemic of a European
disease against which the Indians had no defense. It swept
through the southeastern nations, decimating chiefdoms. In
many cases, taking the lives of the majority of the members of
the Indian population. Food stores had been depleted by
DeSoto's marauding armies, leaving sever shortages.
Paramount chiefs had been undermined by what was seen as
a social and religious failure. Knowledge had been lost as the
elders had died suddenly. Society was without their political,
religious and military leaders. Organization and authority had
collapsed. The people had become demoralized. DeSoto's
short stay set in motion a series of events that brought to an
end the once great chiefdoms of the southeast. Civilization
that had flourished for a thousand years swirled into oblivion
in less than twenty.

"Think, then, what must be the effect of the sight of you and your people, whom we have at no time seen, astride the fierce brutes, your horses, entering with such speed and fury into my country...things altogether new, as to strike awe and terror into our hearts." – Chief of Ichisi, 1540

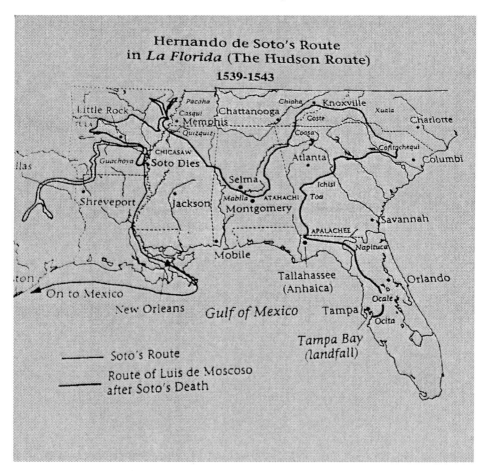

Hernando de Soto's Route
in *La Florida* (The Hudson Route)
1539-1543

Chapter IV

Disease mortality of a magnitude to cause a major population upheaval must inevitably have serious effects on the social organization of any society. But it is particularly hard hitting in a non-literate society that are structured by institutions that are passed on by word of mouth. The people who die in the greatest numbers are often the very old and the very young. And the secondary effect of diseases, including emotional distress and famine, will limit the fertility of reproductive-aged females. This makes the replenishment of populations very difficult. When epidemics are multiple and strike repeated in a virgin population, the result is a pronounced decline in that population. The death of the majority of the old members of the traditional society can only lead to the death of that society's past. Where, in the past, skills, traditions and esoteric knowledge are passed on by the old to the young. Much knowledge may be quickly lost when its bearers die off quickly without the chance to pass on instructions that normally would take years to impart.

The collapse of tradition will occur more or less instantaneously in segmentary tribes where each social group provides its own needs. Everything from household remedies to rules of conduct is a commodity distributed by the specialists. The specialist controls traditional lore and medical knowledge, religious planning and the sacred ceremonial practices. Because this type of knowledge is hard won, it follows its practitioners are most frequently of advanced age and members of an elite. Because this elite has few members and these people are involved in maintaining contacts with other tribes and nations, the likelihood that they will die in an epidemic is greater and that their knowledge will die with them is accordingly high.

Again, wisdom and vision die with the very old and take years to develop in the very young. As the death of the old is the death of the past, so the death of the young is the key of the future. Massive mortality among the society's young can lead to demoralization among those who are left. In addition, in an economy whose productive units are households where the young have significant roles, the loss of these young learners deplete the ability of the household to meet the subsistence requirements and provide for the social interaction necessary to keep it in existence.

When the young and the old are victims of epidemics, the system of kinship itself may be altered. Immediate difficulty arises in the loss of genealogical lore, which is traditionally in the keeping of the old in non-literate societies. When much of the traditional lore of the ancestors is lost, the society will then move towards a more simplified pattern, which is what the Europeans found after the Spanish epidemics devastated most of the Indians of the southeastern United States. This explains why the native Indians disavowed any knowledge of the mounds when questioned by early settlers. "We do not know," was their answer to the query of the origination and use of these earthen structures. In truth, they had lost the knowledge of the existence and purpose of these mounds even though it was their ancestors of less than two hundred years ago who had lived in the areas surrounding the mounds, and who had used them as temple and ceremonial sites.

Historical estimates placed the population of the Indians in the southeast, before contact with the Europeans as high as two million. By 1700, the population of the Native Americans of the southeast had fallen to perhaps one hundred and thirty thousand. Historians estimate that the mortality rate of the epidemics that swept throughout the southeastern United States from 1513 to 1550 may have reached a factor of an 80% death rate. Yet out of the ashes of DeSoto's expedition, and out of the deaths of the pandemics that reigned year after year, 1513 through 1550, there arose a new order. The fragmented portions of the nations and chiefdoms coalesced together to form what would become the civilized nations of the southeast, the Cherokees, Choctaws, Chickasaws, Creeks, and later, the Seminoles, as runaways and slaves would filter back into Florida to remain. Out of the ashes over the next hundred and fifty years would arise the confederations that we know today as the Indian nations.

Language remained a strong unifying force. The Chickasaws, the Choctaws, the Creeks and then the Seminoles, all spoke the Muskogian language. The Cherokee and Tuscarora spoke an Iroquois dialect. The Powahatan of Virginian spoke an Algonquin language, and there were scattered Sioux speakers including the Catawba of Carolina, the Ucci of the coastlines of South Carolina and Georgia, and the Quapaw of northern Arkansas and southern Missouri. An interesting side note was the Biloxi Indians of the coast of Mississippi, who also spoke a Sioux dialect. This was something the early settlers could not understand.

After the French settled the Mississippi Gulf Coast, the Biloxi moved westward to the north shore of Lake Ponchetrain in south Louisiana and then on into central

Louisiana where they merged with some of the Tunica tribes and lost their identity. For a hundred and fifty years after DeSoto left the southeastern United States and the tribes began to come together, they moved inland, away from the major waterways, to escape the marauders that would frequently plow their way through.

Traders trekked through the southeastern interior in the 1600's, no longer looking for gold and precious jewels, but far more prosaic treasure, the hide of the white-tailed deer. White traders soon learned that the skin of these animals, especially the heavy buckskin, brought high prices in Europe, where they were made into luxurious bookbinding and gloves and other merchandise of value. Commerce was something the southeastern people understood and relished. Since the earliest times, tribes of this region had traded with each other. Coastal societies had provided the interior with shells, fish, salt and yopan leaves for brewing the black drink. In exchange, communities form the inland and mountains provided flint for arrowheads, turkey feathers, animal skins and various roots useful for making paints and dyes. For these people, the Europeans were simply new people with different products.

Most of the native communities were eager to acquire these different products. They had metal pots that did not crack. They had knives, hatchets, and hoes that eased the labor of clearing fields and skinning animals. They had cloth for new clothes. Muzzle loading rifles were barely an improvement over bows and arrows for the hunting of deer, because they were so slow to reload. But in time of war, they would terrorize your enemies with their thunderous noise and smoke and fire. To most southeaster people, the exchange of deerskins for these potent weapons and other prized items, was almost too good a deal. But for the most part, commerce worked to the short term advantage of both Indians and whites. It was what came next that did the real damage. By the late 1600's and early 1700's, the peoples of the deep southeast discovered what the natives of the coastal regions had learned nearly a century earlier, that prolonged contact with the whites eventually brought terrible disruption.

Chapter V

For many Indians of the southeast, invasion by the Europeans meant warfare and disease. To some it meant the end of a way of life. To the Natchez Indians it meant the end of everything. The Natchez were the last of the Indians on the Mississippi river who adhered to some semblance of the mound builder, chiefdom type of life. With a population of about five thousand in 1699, when the French came up the river, the Natchez controlled a large territory along the Mississippi River near the city that would bear their name. Their society was highly organized, and formally religious, harkening back to the great cultures that dominated the area before contact with the Spaniards.

The French showed no signs of understanding the reverence the Natchez showed for their ruler and their land. In 1729, the French officials abruptly called on the Natchez to abandon their village so that a French governor could build a home on their site. But to the Natchez, the land on which their village stood was a sacred domain. No white man, no matter how powerful, could be allowed to move them off and live there. In the fall of 1729, therefor, the Natchez attacked the French settlements without warning. Killing some two hundred of the intruders and winning a great victory. But it was not enough. Two years later the French struck back with a large army of Choctaws and other native Indians who regarded the Natchez as their enemies. For the Natchez, it was cataclysmic. Some one thousand men, women and children died defending their village. French slave holders took five hundred others to sell to merchants of the Caribbean. Natchez prisoners deemed unfit for slavery were tortured or burned.

Those who survived fled the area and took refuge with
Chickasaw and some Cherokee native communities.

With a persistence shown again and again by members
of displaced tribal groups, the Natchez refugees managed to
maintain some aspects of their culture in their new
surroundings. Even managing to use the Natchez language
through several generations. But the ancient and majestic
Natchez kingdom that once stretched from St. Louis to the
mouth of the Mississippi died at the whim of an alien empire.

The fate of the several tribes of Florida, if not as that of
the Natchez, was just as bleak. Many of those who had
endured DeSoto's marauding were felled by blow after blow
in the following years by disease and the slave trade. The total
losses were staggering. By the eighteenth century, much of the
lands of Florida were empty. During the early 1700's, various
bands of Muskogian speaking people, most of them Creeks
displaced by wars with white settlers in Georgia and
Alabama, filtered south to take refuge in the deserted empire
of Florida. The refugees adapted to live in this tropical flatland
and gradually the separate bands coalesced into a new, larger
tribal grouping. In effect, repeating the process that produced
most of the major tribes and confederations of the southeast.
By 1775, traditional Creek communities were using the term
"Seminole," (runaways or untamed people) for this new
group in Florida. Some Seminole groups retained their own
language or dialect, but most continued to follow the customs
under local village leaders. Each town grew its own
communal corn crops, for which each individual shared.
Then, a portion was set aside for the local chief.

The Seminoles, themselves victims of the white man, shared their refuge with escaped African slaves. Shared hardships, a common enemy and much intermarriage brought these two cultures together to form what we know today as the Seminole Indians, and a related tribe called the Miccusuke.

A hundred and fifty years after the first Europeans stepped into the southeast, formerly vast Indian territories had been reduced to tribal enclaves. Surrounded by white settlements, the cumulative effect of armed conflict, one-sided peace treaties and outright land grabs, the Seminoles were limited to a tract in central Florida, and the Cherokee clung to the hill country of northwestern Georgia and southeastern Tennessee. In Mississippi, few areas had been open to white settlements and the Chickasaws still held the northern third of the state. The Choctaws retained the middle third with holding extended into eastern Alabama. Yet even those who held onto their tribal identities were much changed from the ancestral ways they had lived.

Most of the small tribes of the southeast, the Tunica, the Chitamacha, the Quapaw, the Caddo, the Yuchee, the Yamasee, the Yazoo, the Chatahoochie, the Acolapissa, the Tuscarora, the Catawba, the Tensaw, did not survive. Most of them were killed by diseases and warfare, or assimilated into other tribes who took them in as refugees.

Chapter VI

Yet contact and commerce again brought about the nightmare of the Indians; European diseases. Traditional treatments had no effect on the new sickness. Poultices and herb and bark were useless against the red rash of the measles which killed Indians by the thousands. The noxious pustules of smallpox were the first signs of almost certain death to the Indians. There was no place for the victims of the communicable diseases. Crowded together in small enclosures only served for the sick to infect the healthy, and the cold bath that usually followed invited pneumonia or other respiratory problems.

In 1738, the disease brought into their country from Charleston, South Carolina by runaway African slaves, one half of all the Cherokee nation died from smallpox. Many who survived committed suicide rather than live disfigured and blind.

In 1828, gold was discovered on the edge o Cherokee territory in Georgia, and the cries for Indian removal began to rise. Later that year, those clamoring for removal of the Indians gained an ally that they needed. Andrew Jackson was elected president. The idea of Indian removal was not new. Years before, Thomas Jefferson advocated the moving of Indians to west of the Mississippi River until such time as they could become accustomed to white ways. Jackson's reasons were of a different sort. He objected to the very existence of Indian nations within the boundaries of the United States.

His security policies meshed perfectly with the land hungry white settlers and their political allies. After a furious debate, Congress passed the Indian Removal Act of 1830 by one vote. The bill allowed the president to give the five civilized tribes an Indian territory, later called Oklahoma, in exchange for the southeastern region that they occupied. That was the carrot. The stick was, that there was a provision in the new law that it could be militarily enforced if necessary.

The Indian removals were to begin with the Choctaws, who were numerous and were prosperous farmers. Andrew Jackson bribed native leaders who persuaded the Choctaws to sign the treaty of Dancing Rabbit Creek. This treaty gave the Choctaw nation land in Oklahoma for all the Choctaw land east of the Mississippi River. The Choctaw, then, were the first to leave their land and to travel the infamous Trail of Tears. In 1834 to 1838 the Chickasaws and the Creeks started on their Trail of Tears. After this came the Cherokees who were to make the longest trek. The Seminoles were rounded up like cattle, loaded onto rail cars and shipped across country, while a small number escaped into the swamps and thus, becoming the Seminoles of today.

Discovery of coal and oil on the Oklahoma land, and the greed of the white man, would again make victims of the Indians who had given credence to the validity of the white man's treaty. The continuing destruction of the Indians moved to a different level when they signed the Treaty of Dancing Rabbit Creek. When they believed the words written in 1830, and signed to by President Andrew Jackson, that promised that, "the land of Oklahoma shall belong to the five civilized tribes for as long as the sun shall shine and as long as the river shall run. Can never be taken away or made a state, or any part of parcel of a state." These words would be repeated in other treaties, and signed to by other presidents. But, sadly, would prove to be repeatedly meaningless in the ongoing interaction of the white man and the Indian.

Laurel Rose Publishing

Laurel Rose Publishing is a small publishing company located in North Mississippi. The company was created as a way for unknown authors to get published and get help in marketing their works. If you are interested in publishing a book and want to know how you can do so contact us at www.laurelrosepublishing.com.

Other Books by Laurel Rose Publishing

Fiction:

Finding Christmas by Ian Johnstone & Chad R Martin

The Blood Queen by S.R. Wooten

Served By Grace by J.B. Jones

Inspirational:

An Inspired Life by Lisa Cockrell

Scriptural Thoughts by Rev Raymond Cross

Why Am I So Happy? by Dr Mike Cockrell

An Uphill Climb by Elliott Bobo

Children's Books:

Our Family by Katie, Ariana, and Chad Martin

Silas' Fall Adventure by Dr Mike & Lisa Cockrell

The Prized Tooth by Prentis Goodwin

The Adventures Of Shawn Shaw Karate Baby by Auntie M

Dad Made A Mess by Shirley Rena Smith

Don't Color On The Wall (Growing with Chloe) by Shirley Rena Smith

Loralai The Lonely by Chad R Martin & Howard Boling

Stanley's Lost Gift by Chad R Martin & Howard Boling

Carson's A Penny Saved by Carolyn Vaughn

Health & Wellness:

Simply Weight Loss by Dr Mike Cockrell

"My Successful Journey" Smoke Free in 14 Days or Less by Hope Crago

Rash Decision Making by Hope Crago

Biographies/Autobiographies:

Suffering For Victory by J.B. Jones

How To:

5 Keys To Publishing On Kindle by Chad Martin & Dr Mike Cockrell

Nature, Gardening, Landscaping:

The Hummer Garden by Lisa Cockrell

Safety:

Life Saving Tips by Hope Crago

Plays:

My Plays: Everyone Should Smile Every Now and Then by James Earl Smith

Poetry:

Treasures of The Heart by James Earl Smith

Stepping Forward: Exploring Nature and the World Through Haiku by James Earl Smith

Wisdom At The Foot of The Mountain by James Earl Smith

Avant 365 by Arthur Avant

The Art of Love by Arthur Avant

Hell's Castaway by Howard Boling

Reaching For The Horizon by James Earl Smith

Searching For The Eagle's Whereabouts by James Earl Smith

A Random Spread of Bones by Howard Boling

Strained Horizons by Howard Boling

To Leave Me For What? By Talvin Grice

Young Writer's Series:

The Apple Thief by The Boys & Girls Club of Northwest Mississippi

Comics/Graphic Novels:

Dynamic Sequence Volume 1 by Nick King

Comedy:

Pooping Scared by Chad R Martin

Audio Books:

The Hummer Garden by Lisa Cockrell

Scriptural Thoughts by Rev. Ray Cross